Records of Disaster:
Media Infrastructures and Climate Change

Future Ecologies Series
Edited by Petra Löffler, Claudia Mareis
and Florian Sprenger

Records of Disaster: Media Infrastructures and Climate Change

Edited by
Jakob Claus and Petra Löffler

meson press

Bibliographical Information of the German National Library
The German National Library lists this publication in the
Deutsche Nationalbibliografie (German National Bibliography);
detailed bibliographic information is available online at
http://dnb.d-nb.de.

Published in 2022 by meson press, Lüneburg, Germany
www.meson.press

Design: Torsten Köchlin
Cover image: Mashup of still from *AAA Cargo*, Solveig Qu Suess,
2018, 34 mins., courtesy of the artist and still from *Ice Cores*,
Susan Schuppli, 2019, 1:06:22 mins., courtesy of the artist
Proofreading: Daniel Hendrickson

The print edition of this book is printed by Lightning Source,
Milton Keynes, United Kingdom.

Printed with the support from Niedersächsisches Ministerium
für Wissenschaft und Kultur (Niedersächsische Vorab).

ISBN (Print):   978-3-95796-208-9
ISBN (PDF):   978-3-95796-209-6
DOI: 10.14619/2089

The digital editions of this publication can be downloaded freely at:
www.meson.press.

Series Foreword:
Future Ecologies

Petra Löffler, Claudia Mareis, and Florian Sprenger

The future of life on Earth has generated ongoing debates in academia, through which the concept of ecology has gained status by being able to connect disciplines across the natural sciences, humanities, arts, design and architecture. Criticism of the effects of climate change, which exacerbate existing inequalities in our global population, has spread from academia to the political and public spheres. At a time when the future of life on this planet is more uncertain than ever, the urgency of exploring other ways of thinking, acting and dwelling together is evident. This book series investigates emerging ecologies in uncertain worlds – ecologies that are open to the interests of other-than-humans and that care for plural modes of existence. By providing a platform for these topics and debates, we hope to contribute to a nature contract with the Earth as the shared common ground of water and minerals, air and birds, earth and woods, living and non-living, active and passive matter.

Future Ecologies is about a "time-space-mattering" that calls into question common knowledges about the relationship between space, place, territory, and the linearity of time in light of the circulation of matter, energies, and affect. It also questions the meaning of past ecologies and unsustainable futures for emergent ecologies, while problematizing the ambivalent histories of environmental knowledge, especially in the interplay of modernity and coloniality. Reading research in the *Future Ecologies* series allows you to take the many facets of past ecological thinking into account, to reveal its differentiated and often contradictory political implications and effects – and to criticize its, sometimes, naïve promises. Studying *Future Ecologies* means not taking for granted what ecology means.

The series promotes a relational thinking that is aware of the environmental, economic, social, and individual complexities of such a pluriverse driven by equally complex technologies and infrastructures. As Donna J. Haraway said, in a shared world "nothing is connected to everything, but everything is connected to something". This connection generates and discloses different scales of responsibility. We dedicate this book series to all earthly critters who want to invent and try out new forms of life and styles of cohabitation, who ask which risks we want to and are able to take, and which futures we dream of. We invite contributions that address the geopolitical inequalities of climate change and capitalist extractivism, that deal with politics of (un)sustainability and (de)futuring, technologies of recycling and environing, non-anthropocentric epistemologies and practices of world-making.

The *Future Ecologies* series advocates for interdisciplinary approaches towards the numerous aspects of ecology. We invite junior and senior scholars from various disciplines in media, cultural and literary studies, anthropology, design, architecture, and the arts to build collaborations between different voices, practices and knowledges – that is: heterogeneous communities of practice. By endorsing open access publishing, the series also aims to partake in the current transformation of the ecologies and economies of knowledge production.

Introduction

Petra Löffler and Jakob Claus

> *The disaster ruins everything while leaving everything intact.* – Blanchot 1995, 19

In recent years, the emergent field of critical infrastructure studies has turned to interdisciplinary analysis of infrastructures as complex worldmaking systems: They produce shared space and time, connect cultures and subjectivities, negotiate power relations, inequalities, or the mediation and circulation of material agency.[1] Infrastructures often appear as networks of media technologies that structure social life and the material world, without much attention paid to them beyond questions of maintenance and failure. We take up this tendency but shift the focus to the recording qualities of both material and media infrastructures in light of anthropogenic climate change. *Records of Disaster* aims to interrogate how environmental disasters manifest and inscribe themselves in infrastructures. In other words, we ask what possibilities and sensory registers of witnessing infrastructures propose and enable as media technologies.

1 See the website of the Critical Infrastructures Studies community: https://cistudies.org/about (accessed July 21, 2022).

Infrastructures are commonly considered to be the stable material and logistical basis of modern mundane life, ranging from electricity grids and sewerage systems to traffic routes and communication networks. While being essential, they are nevertheless subordinated to other structures, social arrangements, and technologies (Star and Bowker 2002). These "life-supporting" subsystems, every-day standards, and reliabilities have in common that they are only actively perceived by their users when they don't work or when they collapse.

It is "the breakdown of infrastructure that opens the taken-for-granted," as sociologists Susan Leigh Star and Geoffrey Bowker have argued (2002, 151).[2] Repeated power outages, network failures, breakdowns of energy supply and communication networks, as well as the collapse of transport routes, logistics, or buildings, due to malfunctioning, material porosity, "human-errors," or military destruction, show that these systems are in fact quite fragile.[3] As architect Keller Easterling states, today infrastructure reaches beyond physical networks of transportation, supply, and communication including "pools of microwaves beaming from satellites and populations of atomized electronic devices that we hold in our hands" as well as "shared standards and ideas that control everything from technical objects to management styles" (2014, 11). This ubiquitous infrastructure is no longer invisible or subordinate – on the contrary, it becomes a medium of power or an "extrastatecraft," (Easterling 2014, 15) in her terms.[4]

The collapses of infrastructures that provide people with water, heat, electricity, food, and information are, however, increasingly triggered by ecological dynamics, changing climatic conditions, and "sudden" events such as forest fires, floods, storms, tidal waves, or droughts. They cause severe damage and suffering at different scales and are classified as disasters when local infrastructural capacities for coping with the event are overwhelmed so that external help is required to overcome the consequences.[5] Such catastrophic events occur because "any system has to cope with an environment that is, by definition, exponentially more complex than the system itself" (Wolfe 2018, 178). Consequently, an increase of complexity on the side of systems or infrastructures as subsystems will also increase the complexity of the relationship with the environment. That is even more the case in a globalized world where people, goods, ideas, and standards are mobilized and connected via networks of transport, logistics, and communication. The Panama Canal for example heavily relies on rainfall and the local ecosystem for its locks to work properly. But in 2019 the annual rainfall decreased, leading to a water shortage in the Gatun Lake, which provides the water to the lock system. Consequently, bigger ships could not pass, again making visible the ubiquitous entanglements between ecosystems, logistics, and supply infrastructure.[6] And the disruption of a local point of interconnected infrastructures will have effects on seemingly disconnected systems and regions – the global is always specific and vulnerable in its locality.

In this context infrastructures are understood as material and communication systems that are planned, constructed, used,

2   Star and Bowker's definition recalls Marshall McLuhan's insight that media are only perceivable as media through the lens of other media. For him, means of transportation such as streets, shipping, or flying routes are environment generating media (see McLuhan 1964).

3   See for example the various reports by the European Commission on the consequences of climate change on critical infrastructure as well as suggested prevention strategies. https://publications.jrc.ec.europa.eu/repository/search?query=Climate+change+and+critical+infrastructure (accessed June 30, 2022).

4   Anthropologist Brian Larkin (2013) proposes a similar approach to infrastructures from a geopolitical perspective, taking dysfunctional or collapsed infrastructures in African countries into account.

5   The United Nations Office for Disaster Risk Reduction (UNDRR) provides a rather schematic definition, which distinguishes between small or large-scale, frequent or infrequent, and slow or sudden-onset disasters. https://undrr.org/terminology/disaster (accessed June 30, 2022).

6   See Fountain (2019) and Rehmsmeier (2022).

and maintained as the interconnected supporting systems of a globalized world. As a signature of the dominant political economy, infrastructures extend toward uncharted territories for resource extraction and potential productivity, such as the Arctic and Antarctic region or the grounds of the deep sea, which have become the site for large-scale infrastructure developing projects. While ecological destruction and climate change manifest as mediated phenomena, infrastructures in their functioning as underlying networks can be understood as seismographs and soft materials of environmental dynamics. Anthropogenic climate change comes to sudden attention by ever increasing "natural" disasters and a changing sensorium for the slow and long-lasting effects of dynamic environmental conditions. Consequently, disaster opens a tension between sudden catastrophic events, that is, fires, floods, and storms on the one side and historically contested evidence such as the slow toxication of ecosystems or the epistemic processes of manifesting knowledge on melting polar caps on the other. In the following we want to propose a critical perspective that makes tangible the ways in which witnesses of and affective relations to anthropogenic climate change are established, structured, prevented, and experienced by what often goes unnoticed.

Approaching Disaster

The term "disaster" is alarming and evocative: it denotes a destructive event that calls for immediate action. Etymologically deriving from the Italian word *dis-astrato*, designating "the state of having been disowned by the stars that ensure a safe passage through life" (Huet 2012, 3), a disaster implies — astrologically speaking — a bad constellation of stars or an unhappy conjuncture of circumstances that causes a catastrophe. However, the secular idea of "natural" disaster emerged in eighteenth century Europe, namely after the fatal 1755 Lisbon earthquake and fire where about 30,000 inhabitants lost their lives. It emerged out of Enlightenment concepts of natural history and the establishment of geology and meteorology on the one hand and of speculative philosophy on the other (Huet 2012). The need to cope with such disasters forced human observers to question the seemingly stable distinction between nature and culture (Hoffmann and Oliver-Smith 2002). Understanding when, where, and why devastating events might occur promised to prevent future disasters. As historians Jason Remes and Andy Horowitz claim, what counts as disaster depends on frames of interpretation, epistemologies, and legal regulations, insofar they are "interpretive fictions" (2021, 2).[7] Depending on these frames, the term "disaster" paved the way to map and interpret such diverse occurrences as floods

7 For Remes and Horowitz "the goal of critical disaster studies is less to understand disasters per se than to understand the processes that create them as ideas, cause them as material facts, and define them as human experiences" (2021, 5).

and earthquakes, famines, epidemics, genocides, and wars. Following philosopher Maurice Blanchot we are aware that our thinking and writing on disaster is affected and at the same time limited by its paradoxical agency ruinating "everything while leaving everything intact" (1995, 19).[8]

There are many reasons to call the present time in Hamlet's words "out of joint," provoking scenarios and narrations of "catastrophic times" (Stengers 2015), a "great derangement" (Gosh 2016), and even "ends of the world" (Danowski and Viveiros de Castro 2016). Not surprisingly, "disaster" is a prominent buzzword in ongoing transdisciplinary debates on anthropogenic climate change, late capitalism, devastated ecologies, and multispecies extinction. For example, art critic and historian T. J. Demos opens his book *Beyond the World's End* (2020) by diagnosing the Anthropocene as the conjuncture of "[c]atastrophic environmental breakdown, global pandemic, neocolonial extractivism, algorithmic governance, disaster and racial capitalism, antimigration populism, and endless war" (2020, 1) while looking for alternative artistic and cultural practices, narratives, and visions for "decolonized futures of environmental sustainability" (2020, 2). In a similar way anthropologist Anna Lowenhaupt Tsing negotiates the disastrous consequences of liberal capitalist economies and ecological violence while asking for new relations with the damaged world we are living in:

The world's climate is going haywire, and industrial progress has proved much more deadly to life on earth than anyone imagined a century ago. [...] And it's not just that I might fear a spurt of new disasters: I find myself without the handrails of stories that tell where everyone is going and, also, why. (2015, 1–2)

However, for Tsing, accepting the precarity and vulnerability of all life and life-supporting systems is necessary to dwell in "capitalist ruins" and to invent ways of collaborative survival and co-habitation in "*disturbance-based ecologies*" (2015, 5).[9] But what is seen and experienced as disaster depends strongly on material and economic conditions and perspective. Or put differently: it depends on one's geopolitical situatedness[10] in a globalized "disaster capitalism" (Demos 2020, 8). Disasters thus need to be (discursively) established as such by recognizing the various ways it affects humans, non-humans, and environments.

During the twentieth century, disaster studies have gained growing attention as a transdisciplinary and collaborative research field in natural and social sciences starting with Samuel

8   Blanchot negotiated the writing of the disaster, which is, for him, at the same time the disaster of writing, that is being in a state of passivity, regarding the twentieth century disasters of world wars, concentration camps, Hiroshima, and the Holocaust as *the* disaster without comparison.

9   Seth R. Reice (2001) also advocates for incorporating disturbance and disaster in ecological thinking to understand how important, depending on their scale and intensity, "natural" disasters in fact are for the biodiversity of ecosystems.

10   We refer here to Donna J. Haraway's (1988) understanding that knowledge is always partial and dependent on the position, perspectives, and interests of the persons involved.

11 Perry (2006) provides an overview on the history of disaster research from the perspective of social science and proposes a definition of disaster as an "area of study" still needing conceptual thinking and structuring classifications. Remes and Horowitz (2021) advocates for "critical disaster studies" informed by humanities methods of interpretation that take modes of imagination and representation into account.

12 The Center was founded by Russell Dynes and Enrico Quarantelli, who has published widely on disaster topics since the 1960s, among others in *Disaster Theory and Research* (1978), *Studies in Disaster Response and Planning* (1978), and *The Study of Disaster Movies: Research Problems, Findings, and Implications* (1980).

13 The EM-DAT website provides a brief guideline of the necessary criteria for a natural disaster to be included in the database. According to this research platform the "call for international assistance" qualifies a catastrophic event as disaster. See https://emdat.be (accessed June 30, 2022).

14 See for instance data provided and visualized by the Center for Hazard and Risk Research at Columbia University, New York: https://ldeo.columbia.edu/chrr/research/hotspots (accessed June 30, 2022) or the annual Global Assessment Report by the United Nations Office for Disaster Risk Reduction: https://www.undrr.org/publication/global-assessment-report-disaster-risk-reduction-2022 (accessed August 23, 2022).

H. Prince's dissertation *Catastrophe and Social Change: Based upon a Sociological Study on the Halifax Disaster* (1920) and sociologist Pitirim A. Sorokin's *Man and Society in Calamity* (1942), among others.[11] In 1963, the Disaster Research Center was initiated at the Ohio State University in Delaware focusing on disasters as social phenomena by studying human behavior on different continents in the wake of catastrophic events and developing operational models to better cope with, forecast, or even prevent disasters by environmental risk management (Rodríguez, Quarantelli, and Dynes 2006).[12] In the humanities, critical perspectives focus on the discursive construction, modes of narration, visualization, and media representation of disasters (Horn 2018, Juneja and Schenk 2014, Passannante 2019, Stubblefield 2015).

Representations of disasters thus manifest in data on environmental catastrophes that are captured and visualized by different institutions. The International Disaster Database EM-DAT, for instance, distinguishes between "natural" and "technical" disasters and collects data on geological or meteorological events such as earthquakes, storms, floods, or fires as well as data on industrial or transport accidents around the world since 1900.[13] The recorded data can be layered onto a world-map showing the unequal distribution of "natural" and "technical" disasters on the globe. As the map (→ 1) suggests, some regions and continents are more affected than others depending on their topography as well as their state of industrialization according to EM-DAT's definition and database. What is to be questioned here are the epistemic framings that render events into disasters, thus again highlighting the political in the "representation" of anthropogenic climate change.

The growing number of extreme weather and geological events primarily perceived and framed as "natural" disasters raise awareness of anthropogenic climate change and its far-reaching impacts on local communities as well as on interrelated economies and ecologies.[14] We understand anthropogenic climate change as a disaster that has all these aspects within its proximity. Following the diagnosis of the Anthropocene condition, the proposed distinction between "natural" and human-made "technical" disasters is no longer plausible. Taking the 2011 Fukushima nuclear disaster as reference point, philosopher Jean-Luc Nancy discusses the interdependency of natural and technical environments: "The complexity here is singularly characterized by the fact that natural catastrophes are no longer separable from their technological, economic, and political implications or repercussions" (2015, 4). This becomes evident as such events leave enduring traces not only

1   Map of the International Disaster Database EM-DAT. (Source: EM-DAT, CRED/UCLouvain)

2   Map of the Global Distribution of Highest Risk Disaster Hotspots by Hazard Type: Total Economic Loss Risks (Source: Center for Hazard and Risk Research at Columbia University, New York)

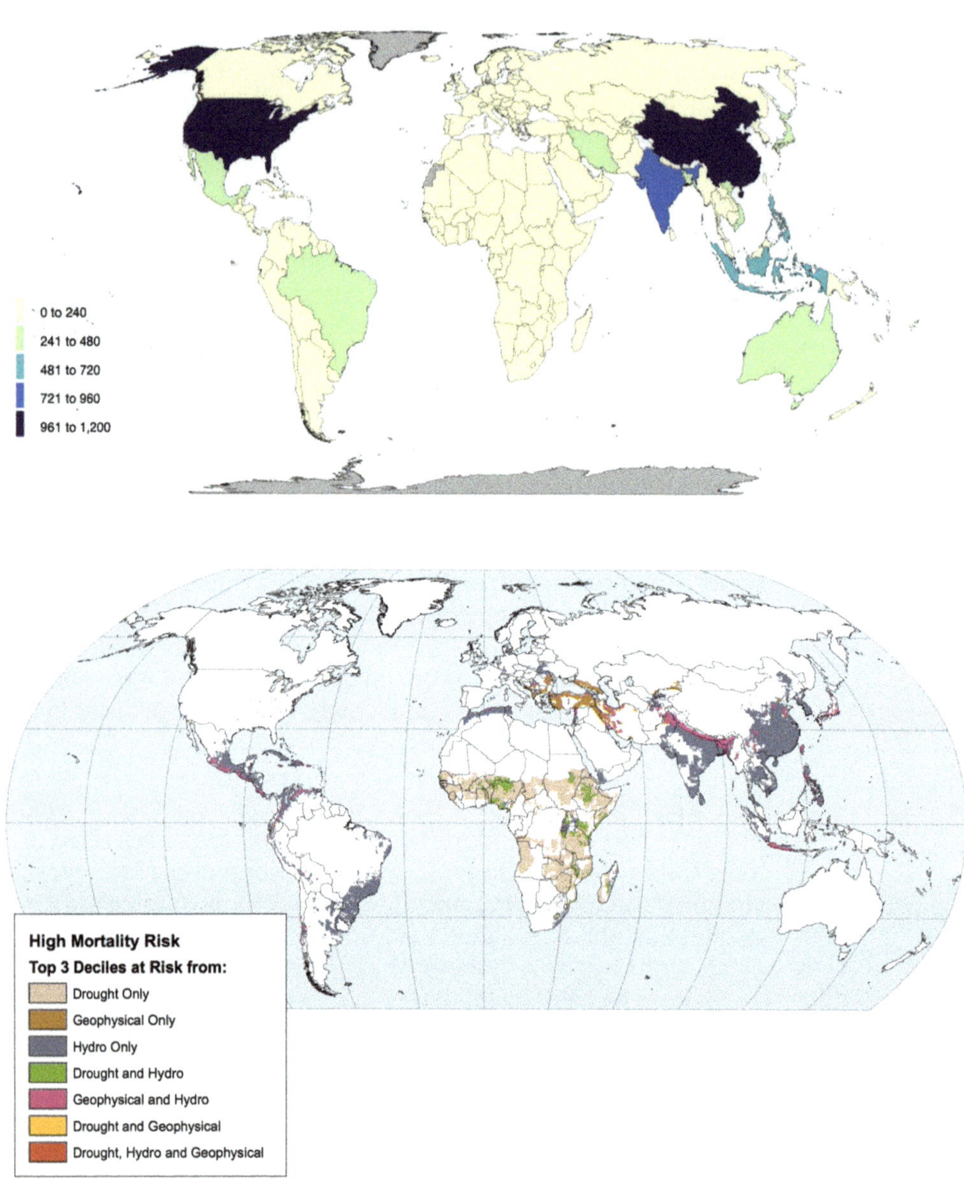

15 The observation that infrastructures span the entire planet encompassing all these spheres has led geologist Peter K. Haff (2013) to envision a global "technosphere" that increasingly functions autonomously, negotiating the negative consequences of human intervention in the global energy regime such as the massive consumption of fossil fuels and the urgency for recycling resources and materials.

within social and economic relations but likewise in the atmosphere, lithosphere, hydrosphere, and biosphere.[15]

However, climate change's many-layered effects are unevenly distributed over the planet along various lines of discrimination and what environmentalist Rob Nixon called "slow violence" (2011). Historically, it is predominantly caused by industrialized states in the Global North, but its effects hit vulnerable communities and infrastructures in the Global South much more drastically, thereby reinforcing geopolitical inequalities (→ 2). "Environmental problems and the people who suffered from them could always be localized, indeed often were in very predictable ways that silently reiterate colonial violence or deepened new vectors of class or racial inequalities," as political anthropologist Kregg Hetherington (2019, 5) has observed. This situation raises serious questions on the ethical and political responsibilities for climate change injustice, as feminist environmentalist Vandana Shiva (2016) has convincingly argued. We agree with cultural theorist Cary Wolfe that "ethical and political responsibility begin with the fact that there *is no* given ground or foundation from which to work, from which the inescapable blindness and partiality of our own situatedness might be surmounted" (2017, 178).

Nevertheless, the common notion of Anthropocene and "the anthropos" neglects the fact that manifold power relations define who is treated as "human" and who or what is excluded from that privilege either as "inhuman" or "non-human" (Gál and Löffler 2021). For historian and geographer Jason W. Moore this "popular Anthropocene is the latest in a long series of environmental concepts that deny the multispecies violence and inequality of capitalism and assert that the devastation created by capital is the responsibility of all humans" (2017, 196). He promotes a historically informed and reflective perspective to think about "the knotty relations of capitalist and planetary crisis" because, for him, the "relations of capitalism and the biosphere are fundamentally interpenetrated" – relations, nevertheless, that "must be historicized and situated geographically" (Moore 2017, 197).[16] For Stefano Harney and Fred Moten, the "transatlantic slave trade, settler colonialism and capital's emergence" constitutive for the modern state appears as "The Socioecological Disaster" (2015, 82).

16 Following historian Fernand Braudel, Moore (2016) proposes "the long sixteenth century" of colonialization of the Americas practiced through resource extraction, warfare, genocide, transatlantic slave trade, and cultural annihilation with its geological detectable traces – the so called "Orbis Spike" – as the beginning of the Anthropocene as new Earth epoch.

We depart from this mapping of disasters and planetary crisis and want to focus on forms, modes, and ways of their manifestation. We thereby do not look at environmental disasters themselves but rather their effects on and entanglements with infrastructures, logistics, norms, and standards on the one hand and colonial histories and presents on the other. Their traces might be inscribed into the soil, which media scholar Katrin Köppert established in reference to feminist environmentalist María Puig de la Bellacasa (2014) "as infrastructure of care" (Köppert 2021, 79). Infrastructure here refers to cultural techniques and practices of transmitting, processing, and distributing narrative pasts and presents. In this understanding, anthropogenic disasters and colonial histories are recorded and kept alive within soil, water, and air. What becomes evident here is the observation that environmental disasters – in their political and economic as well as in their ecological, affective and social dimensions – are to be analyzed in their mediation. We thus suggest turning to infrastructures, their logic, which not only function as breakdown and malfunctioning but also as material witnesses of environmental disasters, to trace at least some of the different layers mentioned above.

Recording Climate Change

The distinctive aim of this volume is to ground these questions and relations to infrastructures as proxies, seismographs, or material witnesses. We borrow the term "material witness" from Susan Schuppli's extensive work *Material Witness: Media, Forensics, Evidence* (2020) to think through the relations that media and material infrastructures record, witness, and render tangible regarding anthropogenic climate change. Schuppli originally introduced the concept to describe the translation processes within legal frameworks that objects pass through to get recognized as evidence in the context of a trial (such as the extraordinary videotape documenting the massacre at Izbica, Kosovo, used as war crimes evidence against Slobodan Milošević). She traces the trajectories of objects that carry a signature of a criminal event in their materiality and follows the processes, rituals, and institutions that transform these objects into evidence.[17] In this respect, the concept carries a double meaning. It refers to a witness that is material to a case. But Schuppli also takes it literally by looking at "material *as* witness," (2020, 10) like the radioactive contamination discovered in Canada's coastal waters five years after the accident at Fukushima Daiichi, or the "disaster film" produced by the oil spill floating in the Gulf of Mexico after the 2010 Deepwater Horizon catastrophe. The concept thus sheds light on how matter is epistemically constructed and fixated on as evidence. In Schuppli's own words: "*Material witness* is, in effect, a Möbius-like concept that continually twists between divulging 'evidence of the event' and exposing the 'event of evidence'" (2020, 3). Schuppli negotiates the consequences of man-made disasters and their relation to the natural world on a geopolitical and juridical level as well as in respect to questions of

17   Schuppli is part of the interdisciplinary research agency Forensic Architecture, established in 2010 by architect and theorist Eyal Weizman together with a group of fellow architects, artists, filmmakers, journalists, scientists, and lawyers. The agency developed counter forensics as a methodology and produces "evidence files" (Weizman 2017, 9) for political and juridical forums such as international courts, truth commissions, citizen tribunals, or human rights and environmental reports. See https://forensic-architecture.org (accessed June 30, 2022).

visuality and knowledge production. We want to extend her concept of "material witness" to discuss the registers and testimonies that large-scale material infrastructures such as marine oil rigs, nuclear power plants, or the Chinese Belt and Road Initiative can display regarding environments and their dynamics. We depart from the assumption that infrastructures, because of their fragility and vulnerability, can be "material witnesses" of environmental dynamics in themselves.

The following contributions continuously negotiate how these "events of evidence" (Schuppli 2020, 3) are conceptually, visually, or verbally captured, mediated, and made sensible for humans. What processes are necessary so that an ice-core can "bear witness" to climate dynamics and the funding infrastructure for climate-research? How does a railway track react to sandstorms and how is this encounter perceived, deciphered, and learned from? We take this concept as a starting point to discuss the relation between infrastructure and anthropogenic climate change and understand infrastructure and logistical networks as evidence and witnesses to environmental dynamics and disasters.

In their conversation with Schuppli, Charlotte Bolwin und Jakob Claus start from her film *Ice Cores* (2019), which is part of the long-term research project *Learning from Ice*, in which Schuppli investigates how scientists interact with arctic ice as evidence bearing material to gain and extract knowledge of anthropogenic climate change. The conversation discusses how disaster can function as an operational concept and needs to be scientifically "fabricated" (in the Latourian sense) in order to be recognized as such. But Schuppli repeatedly emphasizes that, especially in the context of Canadian ice fields and their entanglement with Indigenous people and colonial pasts, the situated perspectives of not only the glaciologists, but herself are crucial for the understanding of ice cores as objects of knowledge. As epistemic objects, material witnesses thereby refer to various pasts without reducing one to the other, or neglecting the social struggles on land in favor of extracting "pure information" on climate disasters. Thus, witnessing opens up the process of institutionalized modes of inscription and fabrication and thus the notion of situated experience and relationality. Schuppli suggests thinking with what she calls "critical proximity" in order to become aware of how ecological disasters are kept at geographical and also affective distance.[18]

Re-thinking Infrastructures
The mediating capacities of infrastructures, as well as their dependency on energy supply and raw materials including

18 Bruno Latour (2005) also coined this term in opposition to "critical distance" to emphasize the necessarily situated site of critique.

19   Jennifer Gabrys (2011; 2016) and Jussi Parikka (2015) were among the first media scholars to have addressed these topics.

waste and toxicity, have become a productive research topic in media studies.[19] Industrial infrastructures are not only shaped by geopolitical interests or are vulnerable to environmental impacts, but must be maintained and repaired continuously, especially after events of breakdown or destruction. That is, infrastructures permanently require labor and care to sustain. The now classical studies of Susan Leigh Star (1999), together with Geoffrey Bowker (1999; 2002) and Karen Ruhleder (1996), among others, have demonstrated in detail that infrastructures need to be continuously maintained, repaired, and their use negotiated. Following their ethnographic methodology, media scholars Lisa Parks and Nicole Starosielski focus on "multiple *media infrastructures*" at the intersection of physical and digital networks such as "data centers," "broadband pipelines, cloud computing systems, digital compression techniques, and protocols" (2015, 1–2). They explicitly pay attention to the histories of media infrastructures as material form and discursive construction in analyzing their "entanglement with environmental and geopolitical conditions from the moment of installation through their residual uses" (2015, 4). The maintenance and reuse of media infrastructures is of special interest here as it reveals a broad field of action.

As cultural theorist Lauren Berlant argues, there is another layer to the nexus of infrastructures „defined by the movement or patterning of social form" and breakdown: „It is the living mediation of what organizes life: the lifeworld of structure" (2016, 393). Thus, the failure of infrastructure renders visible their flaws and draws attention to practices of repair, maintenance, and care. Accordingly, Berlant suggests that a disastrous event and rupture of mundane life unsettles not only infrastructures themselves but moreover the practices of care and repair. When infrastructures fail, "the question of politics becomes identical with the reinvention of infrastructures for managing the unevenness, ambivalence, violence, and ordinary contingency of contemporary existence" (Berlant 2016, 394). The intersection of infrastructures and ecological disasters thus addresses spatio-temporal inequalities, thereby providing a way of re-understanding and re-arranging what is and is not taken care of in modern societies.[20]

20   Curator Bassam E-Baroni dwells on the concept of "infrapolitics" to denote "political acts that lie outside forms of authorized political participation" (2022, 31) in order to negotiate infrastructure as medium and "a kind of 'operating system'" (2022, 31) allowing for "infrastructural critique" (Vishmidt 2017) as well as political action.

The building, maintenance, and repair of infrastructures certainly is time-consuming. Thus, time is integral when discussing the continuous work and activity that is put into planning, constructing, maintaining, or repairing infrastructural systems. Moreover, infrastructural decay evolves mostly unnoticed in a specific time frame according to the life cycles of materials and the continuous effects they have on the environment. In

her contribution, media scholar Gabriele Schabacher addresses the specific temporalities by asking how infrastructures are
"in time." Her focus thereby lies on the disruptive and trans-
forming temporality of accidents and disasters as well as on
the environmental dynamics of geology's larger time scale.
Against this background she develops different perspectives
on the temporal settings of infrastructures in relation to anthropogenic climate change: their processuality, their aging,
and their constitution as a leftover remnant. Schabacher highlights the multi-layered relation between infrastructures and
environmental dynamics. In the case of resource extraction
infrastructures contribute to climate change. But they also
respond to climate change in the form of alternative energies
and mobility technologies. Finally large infrastructural projects
also profit from climate change — for instance in the Arctic
region where the continuous advanced melting of the ice shield
allows for new transport routes and tourism destinations.

What seems to be an advantage for some nations and geopolitical actors certainly is a disaster to others. The melting of the
immense ice shields in the Arctic and Antarctic puts flat coral
atolls and islands under pressure. They must cope with rising
seawater levels besides heavier storms and floods endanger-
ing their very existence. Scientists suppose that coral atolls
such as Takuu in the Pacific will vanish without environmental
protection work and support by the Papua-Guinean government.[21] This is clearly a case of "slow violence" in Rob Nixon's
sense. Starting from the concept of time as continuity, he looks
for the slowly and unequally occurring toxic effects of anthropogenic climate change, what he calls "long dyings" (2011, 2)
and "slow motion-toxicity" (2011, 3). His term "slow violence"
captures "a violence that occurs gradually and out of sight, a
violence of delayed destruction that is dispersed across time
and space, an attritional violence that is typically not viewed as
violence at all" (Nixon 2011, 2). The different and less spectacular time frame of these "slow motion" disasters calls for other
forms of mediation and representation by asking:

[...] how can we convert into image and narrative the disasters that are
slow moving and long in the making, disasters that are anonymous and that
star nobody, disasters that are attritional and of indifferent interest to the
sensation-driven technologies of our image-world? (Nixon 2011, 3)

The urgency to "convert" such not easily graspable and often
ignored disasters into image, narration, and affective reso-
nance is one of the key questions we want to address by turning to the micro-politics of infrastructures becoming material
witnesses.

21   For a represen-
tation of that issue
that takes account
of the perspective
of the Indigenous
Islanders, see Briar
March's documentary
*There Once Was an
Island: Te Henua e
Nnoho* (2010). Nixon
discusses the topic
of climate refugees
referring to the sim-
ilar case of Maldives
Islands (2011, 264–8).

How vulnerable and time-sensitive networked infrastructures in fact are, became evident in 2021 when the container ship *Ever Given* blocked the Suez Canal – the most important shipping route between the Indian Ocean and the Mediterranean – for days. Since then, and in the wake of the pandemic as well as the current war in Ukraine, global supply chains, traffic and transport routes, and logistical networks have come under constant pressure. It has brought these networks and our dependence on a globally interconnected economy into focus. Moreover, politically motivated logistical systems have received increasing attention, most prominently – currently next to the Nord Stream 2 project – the Chinese Belt and Road Initiative that is also known as the "New Silk Road." It is the name for a political and economic paradigm issued by China in 2013 that subsumes large scale investments within around 70 countries and international organizations. The project is not intended to construct a coherent road but a variety of different hubs, ports, roads, and train tracks that enable the movement of goods and cargo. It thereby materializes and expands in many contexts as, for example, the investment and purchase of the Greek harbor Piraeus by Chinese state companies.

Solveig Suess's film project *AAA Cargo* (2018) artistically interrogates the connection between political programs and the planning of the Belt and Road Initiative. At the same time, it sheds light on the lived experience and subversive practices of workers living with, next to, and against the project as well as environmental dynamics that make visible different layers of time. As Fred Moten and Stefano Harney have observed, logistics aims to erase human elements. Moten and Harney provocatively ask:

Where did logistics get this ambition to connect bodies, objects, affects, information, without subjects, without the formality of subjects, as if it could reign sovereign over the informal, the concrete and generative indeterminacy of material life? (2013, 92)

As Suess's work suggests, the aspect of the (resistant) material life of humans and non-humans is hardly ever ruled out completely and inscribes itself continuously in infrastructural systems. The film is thus an artistic travel report from a journey that traced the lines of flight around train tracks, highways, and cargo hubs in China and reports on the various encounters with workers, logisticians, and the environmental dynamics of sand. Together with Jakob Claus, Suess modulated and translated the film into a visual essay, weaving together scenes of the film and its script, thoughts on the aesthetic experience of watching the journey, and relations between logistics and extractive practices.

Counteracting Extraction

Ecological disasters play a crucial part in the sense of the unexpected and long-lasting consequences of global development and the transformation of the planet through omnipresent exploitation of the land and the seas, the extraction of material resources such as metals, minerals, and fossil energies. In her book *The Extractive Zone* (2017), decolonial theorist Macarena Gómez-Barris analyzes the devastating effects of extractive capitalism on different South America geographies and "the ongoing force of colonial encounter" (2017, 2). Not only the land, but also the sea has been and still is an object of colonization and geopolitics. Nicole Starosielski's study *The Undersea Network* (2015) has demonstrated how the ocean and especially the deep sea became a colonized space in the nineteenth century, or rather an infrastructure, where imperial, economic, and scientific interests meet.

Artist-researcher Armin Linke delved deeply into the colonial history of the ocean at the intersection of science and art. In his long-term research project *Prospecting Ocean* (2018) he shows how the vast spaces of the deep sea and the seabed have become an increasingly contested space of extractive and colonial encounters. The almost hidden explorations of the seabed in search of new sources of raw materials are not possible without the massive use of invasive media and technical infrastructures of extraction – from submarines and diving robots to underwater stations and research vessels to production platforms of oil companies and mine operators – which leave permanent traces on the seabed, heavily damaging marine ecosystems and affecting local communities that rely on these ecologies. The footage that Linke used reveals how the seabed is increasingly investigated by remote operated vehicles and cameras operated by marine scientists and, at the same time, colonized by the exploiting practices of deep-sea mining corporations using the same technologies. Linke explores in detail the geopolitical issues of deep-sea mining and current ecological challenges of protecting the ocean and the seabed against their increasing economic exploitation, coloniality, and environmental degradation.

Taking Linke's research project as a nucleus, curator and writer Stefanie Hessler (2019) has reflected on the influence of media and extraction technologies for the geopolitics of the ocean and the deep sea. The conversation between Armin Linke and Petra Löffler follows her insights and scrutinizes the role of media technologies that enter and make visible the immense space of the deep sea. They raise questions on ecology and its relation to material and communication infrastructures as well as on the possibilities and constraints of artistic research and intervention. Their conversation also tackles practices of resistance by Indigenous people in Papua-New Guinea that Linke and his team have experienced during their travels in the Pacific. As his work once more demonstrates, ecological disasters affect peoples and environments in different ways and with different intensities.[22] Climate politics must face the massive inequalities regarding the ecological and economic effects of global warming in the Global South and North, as also historian Dipesh Chakrabarty (2017) has argued. In this regard, infrastructures provide an important perspective that highlights the ways in which colonial trajectories manifest in current dynamics around resource extraction and the destruction of life forms as they inform, enable, and prohibit territories and the movement of people.[23]

Geographer Kathryn Yusoff has addressed the question of ecological injustice by coining the term "Black Anthropocene" as a counterpart to a "White Geology." With these related terms she criticizes the formation of black and brown bodies as inhuman, "organized by historical geographies of extraction, grammars of geology, imperial global geographies, and contemporary environmental racism" (Yusoff 2018, xii). In doing so she points to a blind spot of what Jason W. Moore called the "popular Anthropocence," namely its denial that not all humans contribute to and are not harmed by climate change in the same way and that Blackness is in a "forced intimacy with the inhuman" (Yusoff 2018, xii), that is, the geographical. However, this insight also raises other important questions: Who assumes responsibility and who is willing and able to act and counteract against climate injustice?

Focusing on the blind spots of debates around anthropogenic climate change and climate injustice, Katrin Köppert asks in her contribution why people, especially in Western countries, find it so difficult to connect affectively with climate change and what role the visual politics of anesthetization play in this context. She turns to photographs by the artists Sammy Baloji and David Shongo to discuss aestheticization as an intense and reparative touch that helps observers to affectively acknowledge climate change in its unevenly distributed extent of destruction without mobilizing the desire to restore "pure" nature or landscape. Against Western ignorance and *white* supremacy, she advocates for a "cultivation of affect" and a "reparative reading" of patched visual representations of colonial

22   Anthropologist Elizabeth A. Povinelli (2016) addresses these important questions concerning Indigenous communities in Australia and her collaboration with the Karrabing Film Collective. With Maori scholar Linda Tuhiwai Smith (2012, 6), we acknowledge the problematic nature of the term 'indigenous' and follow her understanding of it as "a way of including the many diverse communities, language groups and nations, each with their own identification within a single grouping."

23   As a recent example of the relation between Coloniality and Infrastructures, see the *Coloniality of Infrastructure: Eurafrican Legacies* conference that took place in Basel in 2021: https://colonialityofinfrastructure.com (accessed June 30, 2022).

histories that complicate the relation between a colonial past as well as a present and a future that is open to transformation. Moreover, Köppert regards the materiality of the photographs itself, based on metal or glass plates and compounds of silver salts, as material witness of colonial extraction.

Capitalist extractivism and environmental violence also play a significant role in contemporary film productions, especially in the so-called "eco cinema" genre or "eco disaster film" (Murray and Heumann 2009). Documentaries that represent issues of anthropogenic climate change and climate injustice mainly through spectacular images, such as Jennifer Baichwal, Nicholas des Percier, and Edward Burtynsky's *Anthropocene: The Human Epoch* (2018), are criticized by cinema and media scholar Jennifer Fay (2022) as "climate disaster porn."[24] Based on the assumption that film is an environmental medium that "reproduces a kind of evidence for a wholly new kind of disaster" (2022, 60), Fay nevertheless advocates for modes of perception and affection that approach these disasters with a sense of responsibility for the catastrophic events depicted. She discusses the potential of audiovisual mass media for generating not only awareness for man-made environmental disasters "we do not fully comprehend as such" (2022, 54), but that ultimately evoke affects and actions.[25] In a similar vein, literary scholar Gerard Passannante reflects on the activating potential of "catastrophizing" in evolving "an experience of the imperceptible mediated by the image of disaster" (2019, 237).[26]

However, the artistic interventions in this volume are primarily concerned with the slow pace of environmental dynamics and the unspectacular audio-visual witnessing effects of anthropogenic climate change and environmental degradation. It is their advantage, with their interest in scientific research methods and in the observational modes of filmmaking, to resist the quest for spectacular images fostered by mass communication channels and to make viewers perceive what they see and hear in terms of a "critical proximity," as Schuppli suggests. With this volume we advocate for mediated practices of witnessing the effects of climate change that take account of the potentials of recording materials as well as the different constraints and entangled actions of humans and non-humans. These practices include concepts of reparation and reparative reading that call for caring and affective response.

Operating Disaster

In the closing roundtable of the workshop, these questions were taken up again and brought into connection. Intended as a closing discussion with the contributors and participants, the

24 With this term Fay addresses film productions that allow spectators to aesthetically approach environmental violence and capitalist extractivism from a comfortable distant position: "not too much disaster and not too much beauty" (2022, 42).

25 Literary scholar Alexa Weik von Mossner (2017) addresses these questions from an ecocritical perspective. See also Fay (2018).

26 Passannante (2019) sheds light on the "making of disaster" as a philosophical tradition connecting materialist cosmologies and speculative thinking, which he refers to as "catastrophizing".

roundtable navigates the diverse contributions and formats and re-focuses on how to think disaster as an operational term and concept. What does it mean to "operate" disaster in times of the Anthropocene? The notion of time is crucial here because in the Anthropocene disasters have become a kind of forecasted and permanent occurrence with a strong impact on future life on Earth. Thus operating disasters requires taking different layers of time into account: first, the interruptive time of the catastrophe; second, the slow motion of environmental disasters that evolve over time, such as ongoing contamination or environmental degradation leading up to destruction or erasure as for example multispecies extinction; and third, the *long durée* of geological time that exceeds the horizon of human experience and existence as becomes evident in the millions of years it took for fossil fuels to materialize, which are then extracted and burned by humans in just a few hundred years. In other words: "operating" disaster now means dealing with these different but intertwined layers of time and space simultaneously, and it means at least staying and living with the probability of and in proximity to the disasters to come.

In addressing the fatal effects of environmental disasters in light of anthropogenic climate change, our suggestions revolve around the observation that disasters do not merely evoke a paralyzed passivity or overwhelming urgency but offer, or better, demand the possibility of resonating with their different effects and renegotiating how to be affected and find ways to (re-)act. Critical proximity to material witnesses and a reparative reading of environmental degradation and its colonial heritage are thus discussed here both as a mode of being distinctively located as well as a form of mediation that testifies and manifests relations between technical media, lived experience, and sensing materiality as witness.

The idea for the book emerged from an interdisciplinary workshop in April 2022 at the Edith-Russ-Haus in Oldenburg and aims to present its diverse contributions. This volume consequently brings together formats including scientific analysis, interviews, and conversations, a visual-poetic essay as well as a roundtable discussion. The workshop presented an honest concern to create a situation that takes seriously the different knowledge practices and modes of negotiating knowledge-production that emerge when interrogating records of disaster. In this context, the artistic research and its various media of presentation that are included in this book hint at an "open methodology" (Biemann 2015, 120). Artist and research-er Ursula Biemann uses this term to describe her approach to ethnographic fieldwork on sites where changing ecologies are observed and captured with visual and audio technologies. The proposed link between media infrastructures and climate change thereby also negotiates transdisciplinary methodologies for the study and analysis of media ecologies that demand an experimental "openness."

We interrogate the mediation of disasters, the role of physical and media infrastructures that focuses attention on their – often neglected or overlooked – interconnectedness with long-term economic and geo-strategic interests without losing sight of their vulnerability and susceptibility to disruption. In short, this volume suggests an analytical perspective on infrastructures as many-layered witnesses of anthropogenic climate change that encompasses interdisciplinary methodologies and brings together scientific as well as artistic research approaches.

Berlin and Oldenburg, summer 2022

We would like to thank the Edith-Russ-Haus für Medienkunst, namely its director Marcel Schwierin, who was enthusiastic about the workshop from the start. Vico Rosenberg and Kristina Wassiljew not only managed the workshop "backstage" but vividly contributed to it "onstage." Arne Wachtmann, Ulrich Kreienbrink, and Mathis Oesterlen gave a helping hand in preparing technical equipment and providing the necessary support. Heartfelt thanks to all presenters and participants at the workshop, our colleagues and students from Carl von Ossietzky University Oldenburg for sharing their thoughts, ideas, and insights with each other. Marie Sophie Beckmann, our colleague at the Institute for Art and Visual Culture, accompanied us in this journey early on and helped us navigating through its turbulences.

We would also like to thank the series editors Claudia Mareis and Florian Sprenger who encouraged us to publish the diverse contributions to the workshop in a volume and accepted the project for the Future Ecologies series, as well as our partners at meson press, namely Marcus Burkhardt, for their patience and expertise. Last but not least we are grateful to Universitätsgesellschaft Oldenburg e.V. and Niedersächsisches Ministerium für Wissenschaft und Kultur for supporting the project financially.

Berlant, Lauren. 2016. "The Commons: Infrastructures for Troubling Times." *Environment and Planning D: Society and Space* 34 (3): 393–419.

Biemann, Ursula. 2015. "Geochemistry & Other Planetary Perspectives." In *Art in the Anthropocene. Encounters Among Aesthetics, Politics Environments, and Epistemologies*, edited by Heather Davis and Etienne Turpin. 117–30. London: Open Humanities Press.

Blanchot, Maurice. 1995. *The Writing of the Disaster*. Translated by Ann Smock. Lincoln, NE/London: University of Nebraska Press.

Chakrabarty, Dipesh. 2017. "The Politics of Climate Change is More Than the Politics of Capitalism." *Theory, Culture & Society* 34 (3–2): 25–37.

Danowsksi, Déborah and Eduardo Viveiros de Castro. 2016. *The Ends of the World*. Translated by Rodrigo Nunes. Cambridge, UK/Malden, MA: Polity Press.

Demos, T.J. 2020. *Beyond the World's End: Arts of Living at the Crossing*. Durham, NC/London: Duke University Press.

Easterling, Keller. 2014. *Extrastatecraft: The Power of Infrastructure Space*. London/New York, NY: Verso.

El-Baroni, Bassam. 2022. "Introduction: Infrapolitics after Infrastructure Space." In *Between the Material and the Possible: Infrastructural Re-examination and Speculation in Art*, edited by Bassam El Baroni. 29–33. London/ Oldenburg: Sternberg Press and Edith-Russ-Haus.

Fay, Jennifer. 2018. *Inhospitable World: Cinema in the Time of the Anthropocene*. New York, NY: Oxford University Press.

Fay, Jennifer. 2022. "Do I Know the Anthropocene When I See It?" *Representations* 157 (1): 41–67.

Fountain, Henry. 2019. "What Panama's Worst Drought Means for Its Canal's Future." *The New York Times*. Accessed July 27, 2022. https://nytimes.com/2019/05/17/climate/drought-water-shortage-panama-canal.html.

Gabrys, Jennifer. 2011. *Digital Rubbish: A Natural History of Electronics*. Ann Arbor, MI: University of Michigan Press.

Gabrys, Jennifer. 2016. *Program Earth: Environmental Sensing Technology and the Making of a Computational Planet*. Minneapolis, MN: University of Minnesota Press.

Gál, Réka Patrícia and Petra Löffler, eds. 2021. *Earth and Beyond in Tumultuous Times: A Critical Atlas of the Anthropocene*. Lüneburg: meson press.

Gómez-Barris, Macarena. 2017. *The Extractive Zone: Social Ecologies and Decolonial Perspectives*. Durham, NC/London: Duke University Press.

Gosh, Amitav. 2016. *The Great Derangement: Climate Change and the Unthinkable*. Chicago, IL/London: University of Chicago Press.

Haff, Peter K. 2013. "Technology as a Geological Phenomenon: Implications for Human

Wellbeing." In *A Stratigraphical Basis for the Anthropocene*, edited by C. N. Waters, J. A. Zalasiewicz, M. Williams, M. A. Ellis, et al. 301–9. London: Geological Society, Special Publications.

Haraway, Donna J. 1988. "Situated Knowledges: The Science Question in Feminism and the Privilege of Partial Perspective." *Feminist Studies* 14 (3): 575–99.

Harney, Stefano and Fred Moten. 2013. *The Undercommons: Fugitive Planning & Black Study*. Wivenhoe: Minor Compositions.

Harney, Stefano and Fred Moten. 2015. "Michael Brown." *Boundary 2* 42 (4): 81–7.

Hessler, Stefanie. 2019. *Prospecting Ocean*. Visual Essay by Armin Linke. Foreword by Bruno Latour. Cambridge, MA/London: MIT Press.

Hetherington, Kregg. 2019. "Introduction. Keywords of the Anthropocene." In *Infrastructure, Environment, and Life in the Anthropocene*, edited by Kregg Hetherington. 1–13. Durham, NC/London: Duke University Press.

Hoffmann, Susanna M. and Anthony Oliver-Smith, eds. 2002. *Catastrophe & Culture: The Anthropology of Disaster*. Oxford: James Currey.

Horn, Eva. 2018. *The Future as Catastrophe: Imagining Disaster in the Modern Age*. Translated by Valentine Pakis. New York, NY: Columbia University Press.

Huet, Marie-Hélène. 2012. *The Culture of Disaster*. Chicago, IL: University of Chicago Press.

Juneja, Monica and Gerrit Jasper Schenk, eds. 2014. *Disaster as Image: Iconographies and Media Strategies across Europe and Asia*. Regensburg: Schnell & Steiner.

Köppert, Katrin. 2021. "Agropoetics of the Black Atlantic." *Zeitschrift für Medienwissenschaft* 13 (24): 77–86.

Larkin, Brian. 2013. "The Politics and Poetics of Infrastructure." *Annual Review of Anthropology* 42 (1): 327–43.

Latour, Bruno. 2005. "Critical Distance or Critical Proximity." Unpublished manuscript. Accessed June 30, 2022. http://bruno-latour.fr/sites/default/files/P-113-HARAWAY.pdf.

Lowenhaupt Tsing, Anna. 2015. *The Mushroom at the End of the World: On the Possibility of Life in Capitalist Ruins*. Princeton, NJ/Oxford, MI: Princeton University Press.

McLuhan, Marshall. 1964. *Understanding Media: The Extensions of Man*. New York, NY: McGraw-Hill.

Moore, Jason W. 2016. "The Rise of Cheap Nature." In *Anthropocene or Capitalocene? Nature, History, and the Crisis of Capitalism*, edited by Jason W. Moore. 78–115. Oakland, CA: PM Press.

Moore, Jason W. 2017. "Confronting the Popular Anthropocene: Toward an Ecology of Hope." *New Geographies* 9 (1): 194–99.

Murray, Robin L. and Joseph K. Heumann. 2009. *Ecology and Popular Film. Cinema on the Edge*. Albany, NY: State University of New York Press.

Nancy, Jean-Luc. 2015. *After Fukushima: The Equivalence of Catastrophes*. Translated by Charlotte Mandall. New York, NY: Fordham University Press.

Nixon, Rob. 2011. *Slow Violence and the Environmentalism of the Poor*. Cambridge, MA: Harvard University Press.

Parikka, Jussi. 2015. *A Geology of Media*. Minneapolis, MN: University of Minnesota Press.

Parks, Lisa and Nicole Starosielski, eds. 2015. *Signal Traffic: Critical Studies of Media Infrastructures*. Urbana, IL: University of Illinois Press.

Passanante, Gerard Paul. 2019. *Catastrophizing: Materialism and the Making of Disaster*. Chicago, IL/London: University of Chicago Press.

Perry, Ronald W. 2006. "What is a Disaster?" In *Handbook of Disaster Research*, edited by Havidán Rodríguez, Enrico L. Quarantelli and Russell R. Dynes. Forewords by William A. Anderson, Patrick J. Kennedy, and Everett Ressler. 1–15. New York, NY: Springer Science + Business Media.

Povinelli, Elizabeth A. 2016. *Geontologies: A Requiem to Liberal Capitalism*. Durham, NC/London: Duke University Press.

Puig de la Bellacasa, María. 2014. "Encountering Bioinfrastructure: Ecological Struggles and the Sciences of Soil." *Social Epistemology* 28 (1): 26–40.

Rehmsmeier, Andrea. 2022. "Panamakanal sucht Wasser. Klimawandel am Nadelöhr des Welthandels." *Deutschlandfunk*. Accessed July 27, 2022. https://deutschlandfunk.de/panamakanal-klimawandel-globale-logistik-100.html.

Reice, Seth R. 2001. *Silver Lining: The Benefits of Natural Disasters*. Princeton, NJ: Princeton University Press.

Remes, Jason A.C. and Andy Horowitz. 2021. *Critical Disaster Studies*. Philadelphia, PA: University of Pennsylvania Press.

Rodríguez, Havidán, Enrico L. Quarantelli, and Russell R. Dynes. 2006. *Handbook of Disaster Research*. Forewords by William A. Anderson, Patrick J. Kennedy, and Everett Ressler. New York, NY: Springer Science + Business Media.

Schuppli, Susan. 2020. *Material Witness: Media, Forensics, Evidence*. Cambridge, MA/London: MIT Press.

Shiva, Vandana. 2016. *Soil Not Oil: Climate Change, Peak Oil and Food Insecurity*, London: Zed Books (second edition).

Smith, Linda Tuhiwai. 2012. *Decolonizing Methodologies: Research and Indigenous Peoples*. London/New York, NY: Zed Books (second edition).

Star, Susan Leigh. 1999. "The Ethnography of Infrastructure." *American Behavioral Scientist* 43 (3): 377–91.

Star, Susan Leigh and Geoffrey Bowker. 1999. *Sorting Things Out: Classifications and its Consequences*. Cambridge, MA: MIT Press.

Star, Susan Leigh and Geoffrey Bowker. 2002. "How to Infrastructure." In *The Handbook of New Media: Social Shaping and Consequences of ICTs*, edited by Leah A. Lievrouw and Sonia L. 151–62. London: SAGE.

Star, Susan Leigh and Karen Ruhleder. 1999. "Steps Towards an Ecology of Infrastructure: Design and Access to Large Information Spaces." *Information System's Research* 7 (1): 111–34.

Starosielski, Nicole. 2015. *The Undersea Network*. Durham, NC/London: Duke University Press.

Stengers, Isabelle. 2015. *In Catastrophic Times: Resisting the Coming Barbarism*. London/Lüneburg: Open Humanities Press and meson press.

Stubblefield, Thomas. 2015. *9/11 and the Visual Culture of Disaster*. Bloomington/Indianapolis, IN: University of Indiana Press.

Vishmidt, Marina. 2017. "Between Not Everything and Not Nothing: Cuts Toward Infrastructural Critique." In *Former West: Art and the Contemporary after 1989*, edited by Maria Hlavajova and Simon Sheik. 265–69. Cambridge, MA: MIT Press.

Weik von Mossner, Alexa. 2017. *Affective Ecologies: Empathy, Emotion, and Environmental Narrative*. Columbus, OH: Ohio State University Press.

Weizman, Eyal. 2017. *Forensic Architecture: Violence at the Threshold of Detectability*. New York, NY: Zone Books.

Wolfe, Cary. 2017. "Critical Ecologies of the Posthuman. An Interview with Cary Wolfe." *New Geographies* 9 (1): 177–83.

Yusoff, Kathryn. 2018. *A Billion Black Anthropocenes or None*. Minneapolis, MN: University of Minnesota Press.

On Cold Matters

and Relations of Critical Proximity

Susan Schuppli in conversation with Charlotte Bolwin
and Jakob Claus

In March 2022, in the run-up to the workshop "Records of Disaster" in Oldenburg, we met with artist and researcher Susan Schuppli to discuss *Learning from Ice*, a multi-year artistic research project conducted in various cryospheric contexts that explores the different knowledge practices mediated by ice to reflect upon our current ecological condition. An adjacent body of work — *Cold Cases* — investigates the ways in which temperature has been weaponized as an instrument of border control and policing against racialized bodies in the US and Canada. Together they consider the epistemic, aesthetic, and ethical dimensions of a material politics of cold. An integral part of these projects is the production of a series of documentary videos that emerge out of field sites at the Canadian Ice Core Archive, the OSU Ice Core and Quaternary Geochemistry Lab in the US, as well as fieldwork in the Svalbard Arctic Archipelago and at Drang Drung Glacier in the Zanskar region of the Himalayas. We invited Susan to reflect upon how her artistic research around climate change negotiates different material infrastructures and environmental communities.

Keywords: Artistic Research, Anthropocene, Climate Change, Documentary Film, Forensic Architecture, Ice, Media Ecology

31

Charlotte Bolwin: Your artistic research project *Learning from Ice* is planned to be pursued for a period of five years from 2019 to 2024. The first part, the documentary *Ice Cores,* which premiered at the Toronto Art Biennial in 2019, gives a first impression on your artistic research practice evolving around the concept of "material witness." In your book on that topic, you describe *Ice Cores* as a media-material case study that demonstrates "the degree to which a rearrangement of matter exposes the contingency of witnessing, soliciting questions about what can be known in relationship to that which is seen or sensed, about who or what is able to bestow meaning onto things, and about whose stories will be heeded or dismissed" (Schuppli 2020, 4). As we learn from your video, ice bears the capacity to inform its audience in various ways. Far from being mute or sterile, your video makes ice conceivable and tangible as a multi-layered spatiotemporal medium – as such indicating or rather materializing a deep climate history; the history of nature-cultures and of human activities as an ecological factor. As your investigation of the Canadian ice core archives shows, ice here acts as a prognostic medium to forecast future dynamics and especially the impact of human actions on our environment, and allows us to read out planetary pasts. Finally, ice is a crucial indicator to prove anthropogenic climate change. We understand the project to further unfold this material agency throughout discursive and media practices as the central concern of *Learning from Ice*. But to begin with, could you briefly describe the video in its relation to the overall project? We wondered: How did you decide to work on this topic, what sparked your interest in ice as a medium and the "politics of cold"? And, as we have mentioned your work on material witnesses already, what theoretical considerations have gone into this video?

Susan Schuppli: The *Learning from Ice* project, in effect, continues the last chapter of my book *Material Witness*, which started to make an argument around what I called "earth evidence," although the book begins with an inquiry into what we would understand to be conventional notions of media: film, photography, video, and audio recordings. I then unfold these media artefacts, all of which are in some ways evidential, over the narrative arc of the book to examine the ways in which materials come to bear witness or are mobilized within contexts in which they can testify to events. In my research, these events often tend to be conflicts in which violations of one kind or another have happened. However, in developing the concept of the *Material Witness* over many years I also expanded my understanding of what could be considered a media artefact or a form of media (Schuppli 2020).

By the end of the book, I am really exploring unconventional notions of media materiality. For example, an oil spill, or oil film as its technically called, in the Gulf of Mexico that was a consequence of the Deepwater Horizon accident. In that chapter I made an argument that nature was capable of representing itself by virtue of its own technicity, which resulted in modes of expression which are decidedly mediatic. In doing that research, I also started to look at what I call data proxies. A data proxy is something that offers an indirect mode of measurement of an event or an external condition. A tree ring is a data proxy because it can tell us something about the conditions of precipitation long before the invention of scientific instrumentation. Ice cores, too, are data proxies.

An ice core is a vertical column of ice that is extracted from the ice sheets using drill technology. This ice sample contains the atmospheric relics of our ancient climate history. I was really compelled by ice cores, which are paradigmatic examples of "earth evidence." In ice cores you can access air bubbles containing greenhouse gases – for instance CO2 or methane – that were deposited on the glacial ice sheets hundreds of thousands of years ago. Because ice cores contain the actual material residues from another time, they have been able to provide key evidence proving that the warming of the planet has exponentially increased since the industrial revolution. Ice, when subjected to specific technical probes and analysis, thus becomes a *material witness*.

My first encounter with the Canadian Ice Core Archive at the University of Alberta was via a news article reporting that the newly built state-of-the-art facility had experienced a triple malfunction. Instead of keeping the cores at minus 25 to 30 Celsius the freezer temperature spiked, soaring to plus 30 degrees Celsius.[1] Over the course of one weekend thousands of years of climate history, specifically Arctic climate history, literally melted away. I was provoked by that story, but also it was the first time I realized that Canada had an ice core archive. As someone who is Canadian, I found this amazing and thought that I would really love to visit the archive to document the work of the scientists there.

Jakob Claus: This is an interesting point that leads to another question about the production conditions of the video: an ice archive has temperatures far below zero. What might be a comfortable temperature for human beings would be the destruction of the sampled ice cores; everything would melt away as it happened in Alberta. The fact that there is enormous artificial cold in the ice archive seems quite obvious and hardly worth

1   See for example Colette Derworiz (2017).

mentioning. However, watching your video in its calm images and even meditative settings we sometimes tend to forget that the shooting of your video took place under extreme conditions – precisely sub-zero temperatures that protect the ice from melting away before they have been classified and examined. While melting in fact is an essential process to scientifically "read out" the information that the ice contains and allows for insight in the deep time of climate history and climate change, keeping things cold is an integral condition for an archive of frozen matter. So, as your video takes us to the realms of the polar zone and to cooling chambers artificially reproducing temperatures far below zero, we wondered: How did this site-specific condition impact the production of the video? How did you organize your research and prepare for the shooting on-site, inside and outside the lab, and for recording image and sound? Put differently: How did the media apparatuses interplay with the environment?

Susan: That is a super important question because, of course, most technological instruments are very sensitive to temperature at either end of the spectrum. For many of these projects I have worked with a former MA student, Henry Bradley, who is an artist in his own right. One of the first things that we did was start to reach out to people who had been working as filmmakers, doing field recordings and shooting in cold environments. So it always needs to begin with pragmatic research. Preparation is key in embarking on these kinds of projects and in working in these extreme environments.

Digital technology in particular is very susceptible to cold for a number of reasons. The first is battery power, which is radically diminished. Batteries drain very quickly in cold environments. If you don't have the power to power your technology, your shots are lost. But at the same time, you also need to plan the ways in which you move equipment in and out of different temperature zones. You have to avoid moisture build up inside the instrumentation. For example, in the case of filming in the ice core archive, we would film for about say 45 minutes at a time. If you are working on a camera, you can't really use bulky gloves, so your fingers have to quickly come out of your gloves to adjust your aperture, etc. It was in fact shockingly cold because there is a complete lack of humidity in the ice core archive. It was this incredible kind of penetrating cold. Your own body has to manage that condition at the same time that you are trying to manage the recording technology. But what it meant was that after a period of filming – usually filming for the duration of a battery, which lasted about 45 minutes – we would have to take the cameras out of the ice core archive, out of the freezer, and wait for two or three hours for the cameras to slowly adjust to the different temperature before we could then go back inside. So it is not a situation where you can run back and forth, "oh, I forgot this or that, I am going to quickly dash outside and come back in." Everything has to be planned and it takes a lot of time. I think anyone who has shot a video knows this; setting up shots, setting up your equipment, all this really takes a long time. That can especially be a challenge when you access laboratories – places where people are working, because sometimes people don't realize you are going to be there for a while in their workplace. It requires preparation from me as a filmmaker, but also patience and generosity on the part of the scientists and lab technicians with whom I've collaborated.

Charlotte: Following what you already told us about your concept and production contexts, we would like to address the specific audio-visual aesthetics your video applies. We ask this with regard to an aesthetics that is in once sense representative, but also reaches further and opens up a sensorial space where the medium itself is not merely transparent, but allows for a certain ambiguity and a specific density that enables aesthetic experiences. Against that background, one could connect your practice not only to the epistemic processes of the laboratory – documentation and archiving – but also emphasize the aesthetic impressiveness with which your video comes up on the level of image and sound; the sensual and perceptive realms it opens. Here, a tendency of contemporary artistic projects seems to become visible: the politically and ethically informed concern to bring theoretical configurations such as the discourses around Anthropocene back to specific experience. Besides what has been paradigmatically called an "epistemic turn" (Holert 2020) of the arts, there also seems to be an interest to engage artistic practices to mediate "disturbing times" (Haraway 2016, 1). As Timothy Morton (2013) has stated, the words and concepts we have at hand to describe the shifts of our present, such as global warming and climate change, thereby tend to give us the slip – they remain abstract and elude lived experience. Could we then also understand a video like *Ice Cores* as a sort of sensual ethnography from and within the field that not only wants to tell but allows for an affective, bodily encounter through the coupling of materials and media technologies?

Susan: Certainly, these are considerations that come into play when you engage with a material like ice, which is both extremely ordinary in the sense that we probably all have some relationship to it within a domestic context. At the same time, it is also an incredibly extraordinary material. It has a certain spectral quality, in terms of its transmogrified nature: undergoing constant change through melting. It also tends to elicit a melancholic response, which I have to say, isn't something that I am personally committed to. Put differently, it is an integral part of the contemporary story of ice, but I don't want to stay in the melancholic register when it comes to researching and learning about glaciers and melting polar ice caps. So the challenge is how to produce work that is both affective but also generates critical debate about the future, rather than that which merely mourns the loss or passing of ice. Moreover, I think, what is important for people to understand is that not just viewers of these films and creative projects, but the scientists themselves who work with these materials have an affective and empathic relationship towards ice and the life worlds it is part of. Professor Edward Brook, who appears in the *Ice Cores* video, is the director of the *OSU Ice Core* and *Quaternary Geochemistry Lab* where they do greenhouse gas analysis. At one point, Ed was saying that he sometimes just takes time to look at the ice sample in his hand and reflect upon where it was sampled, how it was taken out of the ground, how it was measured, etc. – the field context out of which the material emerged. In other words, he spends time with the material, engaging with it at the level of its sensorial properties, which are in excess of its purely scientific use value.

It is not that scientists just approach these materials through the paradigm of objectivity. These are the objects of their research inquiry and their task is to extract the data, which will ultimately be transformed into information and make its way into the environmental policy documents that are discursively translated across a variety of domains. Yet scientists themselves have a deep affection, I would argue, for the materials of their research, and it is likely the thing that brought them into that field in the first place. One is not simply born a scientist, one becomes a scientist through a set of long-standing interests that often arc back through to one's childhoods. And a lot of those interests, I think, have a strongly affective dimension. For me it's really important to emphasize this because sometimes I get the impression that artists tend to caricature the world of science. Or at the very least reduce its complexity to the domain of objectivity in opposition to the domain of affect and sociality. These relationships are much more complicated when thinking about a "sensory ethnography."

Because I am trying to denaturalize the images I capture and make, I am trying in some way to attune myself – to use the term – to the dynamics of matter. I need to work with different microphones, different lenses, etc. to try and maybe register conditions that are not always perceptible within the realm of human vision and hearing. I use highly sensitive microphones that can sense extremely low frequencies – the sound of air being released by melting ice. I have also worked with a thermal camera but that was a bit more challenging, I have to say, as I wanted to work with a different camera whose very organizational principles were thermostatic. It was an experiment, but I can't say one that was completely successful. So I am trying to develop visual and acoustic languages using different sensors and sensing technologies to expand or open up the frequency range. And the reason for that, of course, is, as Timothy Morton has said, that a lot of the things that we are dealing with challenge the thresholds of human perceptibility. They are not organized around human modes of visuality or audition, let alone human modes of temporal understanding. Thus, one has to develop different strategies and ways of working. I hadn't thought about it previously, but in following my interest in the data proxy, we could perhaps say that the film or video has to become some sort of proxy that attempts to mediate these different conditions of perception. Of course, I am making something for which the viewer of the project will be a human. So ultimately, I need to translate the a-visual and an-acoustic elements of the scene into something that has in some way captured what is at stake. I want to produce an image about something that I am arguing is in fact in excess of the visual or in excess of the acoustic – that in short exceeds representation. And yet I have to narrate it and try to turn that condition back into something that we can see and hear. That is the fundamental paradox of my work.

Jakob: As you indicate, sound plays a crucial role in activating the affective dimensions of the audio-visual. This is certainly true with regard to your video. The audio is a key aspect of the haptic visuality and the general experience that one has with the materiality of ice. Ice becomes a powerful medium especially as it sounds, even if this tone is additive or belongs to the infrastructures in which the politics of cold are embedded. It makes us think of Gilles Deleuze (2006), who states that "forces" are something that can or must be made audible to be perceived and understood. Of course, Deleuze's philosophy could be invoked here overall, as he argues that the moving image has the potential not simply to represent the vividness of reality, but that film is an aesthetic medium that amplifies and expands the reality it captures. Deleuze (2004) uses "dramatization" as a method to access and focus on the qualitative aspects of phenomena considering the multiple where, when, and how instead of asking the metaphysic questions what and why. Would you agree that audio-visual forms have a special capacity for such alternative ways of relating to reality and to objects, infrastructures, and more-than-human surroundings?

Susan: It is interesting that you invoke Deleuze on dramatization here. That is something that I was really interested in during my PhD – his concept of dramaturgy and the challenge to think about the ways in which materials come to stage different kinds of encounters between stakeholders and communities; between different forums and interest groups but also between different sensory registers. In *Ice Cores*, the images might seem relatively stable and recognizable. They are documentary in a very conventional way. But yes, the sound is telling us that there are other dynamics at play, something that we cannot fully access through the visual register. I use the sound to subvert the image track, if you will. To alert the viewer or the listener to the fact that something else is going on. What it is exactly is not always completely clear.

Sound has the capacity to trigger the psychological realm in a very persuasive and convincing manner. In *Ice Cores*, it was important to me that the sound could somehow account for the lively internal world of ice, that these cores were not simply mute and silent witnesses, waiting in the archive for that moment when they would be extracted and come to life through the intercessions of the scientist. I tried to create the sense that these ice cores were somehow lively, rather than inert, matter, and so I worked on developing the transmissional qualities of the ice cores... to consider ice as a kind of medium that was transmitting the signals of climate change. I therefore needed the sound to do some of that conceptual work for me.

Charlotte: Since its beginnings, documentary film theory has extensively dealt with the tension between a creative use of sound and a recording and reproduction of original sound that is as true to reality as possible. Your video combines both, on-field sound and a musical score you produced especially for this project. And there is the voice-over which accounts for a distinctive auctorial perspective, as it is your voice that we hear. Could we say that the intertwined sound layers refer to different forms of documenting and witnessing? And what is the role of speech and your own situated voice in this video?

Susan: Well, there are some very practical responses to that question. First of all, the project was shot in Canada where I grew up; I have a Canadian accent. So, it was a purely pragmatic decision as I needed someone who had a Canadian accent. I did not want it to have that classic English BBC-type of voice. I wanted the voice to be situated culturally within the film's context. On the other hand, when I am trying to tell a very complicated story I tend to rely on my own voice since I have an internal voice in my head that is shaping the narrative. That being said, I do a lot of writing beforehand to organize my ideas. Although I make a sustained argument around the agency of matter in my book, one could say that I speak on behalf of materials in my artworks. My own personal challenge as an artist is thus to try and reduce the necessity for a voiceover and find other modes of narration.

As you mentioned, I worked with a composer who produced the musical score. I always produce the sound design for my projects even when I am working with a composer or with a musician. While working with Mohamad Safa for *Ice Cores*, there was an Estonian jazz musician that I really liked and so I scored the video initially using his music to give Safa a sense of the kind of ebb-and-flow as well as melodic shape that I wanted. Safa always creates his own compositions, but at least we had some sort of template for imagining the sonic structure of the piece.

Finally, the role of the field recordings is quite essential. In an earlier project, I developed a strategy that I like to return to. It was a film on nuclear radiation[2] and we (sound designer Philippe Ciompi and I) decided that every sound would originate from a different source than what you see in the image. Throughout the film we hear the Geiger counter – that classic clicking sound – but that sound was produced by a very specific whale that emits a very similar clicking sound. It was a strategy of sonic displacement that we felt could do something on a subconscious level. I'd like to do this again: to create some tension between what we think we are hearing and what we are actually hearing. Developing different sonic strategies is really crucial to me.

Jakob: Another aspect that brings us back to the content level is how you depict different kinds of labor. First of all, and we talked about this with regard to the conceptual approach of your video, there is the activity of materiality; the ice that performs actions of encoding and decoding and is exposed to or activated by various processes of transformation throughout the operation chains of the laboratory. But in the lab, there are technical apparatuses and human bodies. As your video shows, all these agents work closely together and form situational entanglements. At the same time, your video makes the gaps or boundaries visible that lie between the different working steps, so that individual gestures and operations stand out clearly.

2   Susan is referring to her work *Trace Evidence* (2016).

We found this displaying of labor a very remarkable aspect of your video, especially if we understand it as a documentary approach. There are so many scenes that observe the scientists at work; they are shown as they move through the lab, move the ice, check on cooling, measure values, unpack, pack, cut, and categorize the material. As we watched the video we apparently stumbled on the numerous hands that are appearing within different gloved constellations. These somehow structure the images and relate the different registers of human and non-human activity. If we step back from the conceptual and focus on the content layer, we become aware that your video is, besides everything else, tracing labor: the labor of the materials as well as the (manual) labor and activity of the scientists and of the machines supporting and enabling this work. What role did this dimension play for the research on ice and how would you describe your artistic approach to that?

Susan: It's funny that you mention the hands. Something happened when we were shooting the video in the lab in the United States. Because there were no women working in the lab, I said to the cameraman Henry at one point that I can't just make a documentary full of male subjects. Henry took that as a cue to focus on hands, not to show people talking, but to always direct the camera away from faces towards the moving of hands. When I was doing the editing, I did have, let's say, a disproportionate amount of footage of people working on dials, on instruments and pointing things out. And that was in part a consequence of a lack of communication and direction between myself and Henry. That being said, yes, it is very much a meditation on labor as well. In answering one of the other questions, I talked about the ways in which a filmmaker like Chantal Akerman is a very useful point of reference for me, precisely because her films can really be characterized as a kind of meditation on the minor dramas of the everyday. I think that is a description of her work that I read once and so this idea of a meditation on the minor dramas of the everyday has really stayed with me. I am interested in the labor practices that are necessary for understanding materials such as ice and consequently the claims that can be made with these worked on materials. But this all takes time.

I also realize that looking at processes unfold in real time is challenging for viewers, because we don't have this as part of our contemporary cinematic condition anymore. I was endlessly fascinated when Alison Criscitiello, the glaciologist, was working on a very long ice core in the freezer, brushing and scraping it. I could watch that for the whole two hours that it took to prep, but of course I had to cut down this scene considerably in the video. Yet I just found it endlessly fascinating. The very attentive ways in which she was handling the ice core, turning it around, brushing and moving it; the ways that she was looking at the material, trying to understand it. These are practices of care, in fact, that are being mobilized by the people working with these icy materials. To me, that is really important. It needs to be part of the story. But I realize it also doesn't always make for a compelling narrative.

Charlotte: In your video, you also refer to the political dimensions of the archival and scientific practices in the Arctic — both, inside and outside the lab. The area we are entering with your video, the area where the field research for the glaciology is conducted, is the Canadian ice fields. These fields are part of a sensitive territory with a manifold history as a natural space but also as a cultural site in which colonial history is inscribed. While it is in the interest of climate scientists and ecologists to recover and study the ice, at the same time the question arises: what do the interventions and extractions that are part of the depicted research and archival practices mean for local communities and Indigenous groups. At one point in the video, you mention the environmental stewardship program and the Nunavut Research Institute as institutions that can give or can refuse permission to work and do research on the land.[3] Compared to other forms of scientific extraction, the drilling of ice cores appears as a rather low impact extraction. Yet still, the production of knowledge and data entails responsibility. You already spoke about the question of situatedness and the knowledge of local contexts for such kinds of artistic research projects. As it becomes clear in various scenes throughout the video, the scientists also operate in a sensitive and conscious relation to their field. Could you say something about how the researchers you met would respond to these questions? And how do you position your own artistic research practice within these politics of fieldwork?

Susan: These are crucial points. As Alison Criscitiello explains in the video, in the Canadian context, in terms of working in Nunavut, the most important permission that you can get to do your work there is the permission from the local Indigenous community, which is to say, the permission to work on their land. Even with something like ice coring, which seems to be relatively low in terms of environmental impact, the point is that land is being worked on and disturbed in some way.

In relationship to the cryosphere more generally, an ethical debate is emerging around the assumed right to break sea ice by ice breakers. The life worlds maintained by ice floes are fragile

3   See the website of the *Nunavut Research Institute*: https://nri.nu.ca/ (accessed June 20, 2022).

Stills from *Ice Cores*, Susan Schuppli, 2019, 1:06:22 mins., courtesy of the artist

SPC 15
Box 14

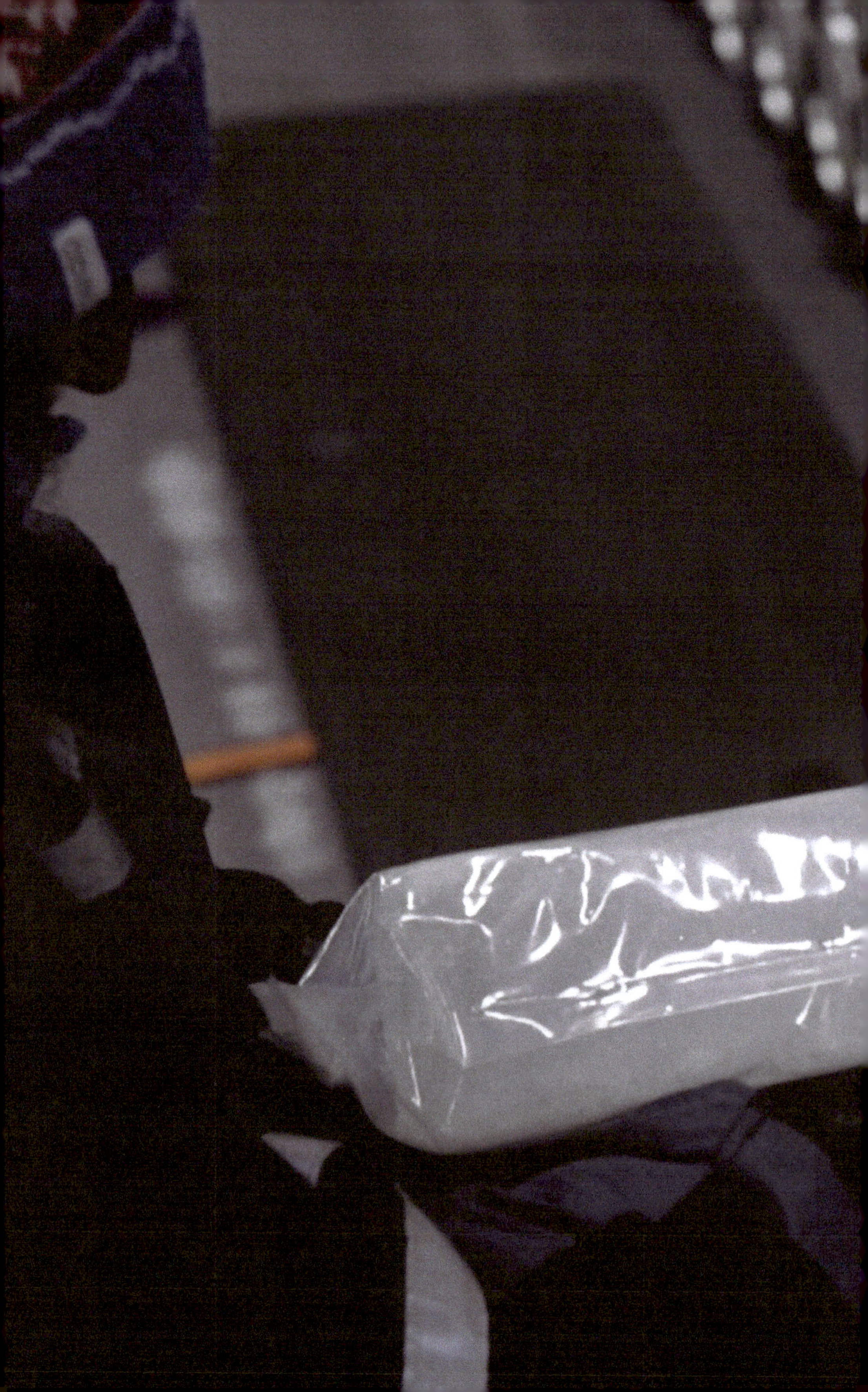

TOP →

Scotia
TCN
N K S
JEL-028
BYRD
BYRD
PROTECT FROM HEAT
ICE CORES
MAINTAIN TEMP AT -20C
KEEP FROZEN
ICE CORE
MAINTAIN TE
AT -20C
KEEP FROZ

JP04
BOX 34
ARCHIVES
KEEP FROZEN
DESTINA
NIC
PERISHABLE
HANDLE WITH CARE
PROTECT FROM HEAT
CORES
MAINTAIN TEMP AT -20C
KEEP FROZEN
Se JEL-033
KAH
NSF CONTRACTOR REP USN-CBC
BLDG 471 NORTH END
PORT HUENEME, CA 93041
ATTN: JACKIE SAMUEL
NATIONAL ICE CORE LABORATORY
BUILDING 810, USGS
BOX 25046
DENVER FEDERAL CENTER
DENVER, CO 80225
ICE COR
MAINTAIN TEMP AT
KEEP FROZEN

SUM14
OSU
2014
SUMMIT
PETRENKO

HEAVY
HEAVY

NSF CONTRACTOR REP USG-CRC
BLDG 671 NORTH END
PORT HUENEME, CA
ATTN: JACKIE SAMU
N64497-VSG-AW
WT /83 CU #

NATIONAL ICE CORE L
BUILDING 810, USGS
BOX 25046
DENVER FEDERAL CENTER
DENVER, CO 80225
ATTN: I-355/COLE-DAI

ICE CORES
MAINTAIN TEMP AT -20C
KEEP FROZEN

Sensitive

KAH-009

PROTECT FROM HEAT
23
N64157-4054-H015-XXX
DRS
5100
PPM SAMPLES: ICE CORES

KEEP
FROZEN

Sensitive Product
GISP

DESTINATION
NICL

HEAVY
HEAVY

SISP 2

ICE CORES

Temperature Sensitive Pro

and in need of practices of preservation and care, yet this has not been part of the broader climate story when it comes to thinking about the changing material conditions of cold. Lastly, this is really a question about ethics. What are my own ethical responsibilities in producing these works, which in some ways are extracting images and extracting ideas? I interact with other people, and their voices, their practices, their knowledge becomes part of my work. There is definably a certain extractive dimension to almost all forms of cultural production. For me it depends on the kind of relationships of trust that one establishes with the people that you engage with. And I am not talking about the sort of standard protocols that researchers have to abide by, where they have to tick off an ethics form. I am thinking about an ethics of engagement that accounts for our own situatedness within these sorts of contexts.

Jakob: As you describe in your book *Material Witness*, documents as objects need to go through long and institutionalized procedures to become witnesses of an event such as climate change, war crimes, or ecological damage. In *Ice Cores* there seems to be a similarity concerning the process of fabricating facts and data, of rendering the ice informative. Regarding science and technology studies and the sociology of knowledge, one could understand these processes as the constitution of what Bruno Latour (1999) designates as "circulating references." Latour discusses the constant negotiation, translation, and balancing between concrete materiality and abstract information values that come into play in different contexts of social and epistemological processes of cooperation. *Ice Cores* shows how the relevant locations for the cores are chosen, how the cores get drilled, stored, cooled, selected for analysis, and respectively are processed, cut, stamped, scanned, visualized via technologies that unfold the data and hence knowledge. As you agreed earlier that one aspect of your video is the documentation of labor, we were wondering how you portray and interrogate the relationship between human and technological activity with regard to what you call "earth evidence"? How do you unfold the "experimental system" (Rheinberger 1997) that is evidently at work?

Susan: I have always been fascinated with these moments of translation. In the opening sequence of the video, we see the ice moving through a series of transformations en route to becoming data. This is the overall narrative arc the video traces: how the ice ultimately becomes a discursive object that gains its political relevance within the context of environmental policy debates and climate change forums. Edward Brooks addresses this process at the very end of the video – and somehow responds to what you just described. Ed is convinced that the chemists in the lab need to have a sense of the overall context in which they are working. They need to understand where their own research materials are coming from and the thousands of things, decisions, experiences, activities that are part of this "dramaturgy" – in short, the pre-conditions of their work – such that they can separate water and gas in a laboratory. Labor practices are always part of a much larger assembly, but it is often difficult to have a sense of where we plug into these networks. We often only have partial knowledge, yet I think to understand the politics at play one needs to be able to somehow crack that larger picture. That being said, I recently talked to a climate scientist in Bergen, Heiko Goelzer, who models ice sheets, specifically the ice sheets of Greenland. He told me that he doesn't go to "the field" i.e., Greenland. He works with the data extracted from there, but his field is a computational one. Even if Goelzer's fields are computational, he still needs to understand their computational infrastructures, I would argue. How is the global climate model built? What decisions are being made before he gets to work on the data, how is data being correlated across data points? It is important for me to have an extensive understanding of what constitutes a field in someone's practice.

Jakob: When we conceptualized the workshop *Records of Disaster*, we thought of disaster as a certainly challenging but operational concept to contrast different perspectives on catastrophes, environmental change including their material, social, political, and historical dimensions. One reason we invited you to discuss and screen *Ice Cores* is your long-lasting and continuous work on the dynamics between environmental change, natural-cultural history, agency, and a sense of urgency that especially marks this project. Similar to what you already mentioned concerning the oil spill as medium – as shown in your previous works *Nature Represents Itself* (2018) and *Disaster Film* (2019) – you approach ice cores as a medium with different recording qualities or registers. First, there seems to be a more or less passive recording quality of ice that is inscribed with environmental change and deep time. Ice is a slow medium that needs time to unfold its archival potentials both ways: the slow enclosing of particles and molecules as well as extracting them again. But at the same time, ice can display sudden political or social events such as the Partial Nuclear Test Ban Treaty,[4] which unintendedly became a means of calibrating ice cores. And second, there is an undoubted fragility of ice as a storage medium, as it can easily melt, break, or just be accidently interchanged, which would result in confusing timelines and taxonomies. How did you encounter the

4   The Partial Nuclear Test Ban Treaty is an arms control agreement on the testing of nuclear weapons, signed in 1963 by the Soviet Union, the United States of America, and the United Kingdom. By 1964, more than 100 states had joined the treaty as signatories. While as of 2015 over 120 states have signed it, 60 states – including China, France, and North Korea – have not. See: https://treaties.un.org/pages/showDetails.aspx?objid=080000002801313d9 (accessed June 20, 2022).

aspect of time in the interplay between ice as material and film as medium?

Susan: There is so much temporal complexity at stake when we are talking about ice cores and the filming of them. Ice is a material archive in that it records atmospheric events and then this material archive becomes part of another archive; an ice core archive. Every film frame too is an encrypted archive, so when I film an ice core archive it's a further multiplication of the archival process. But pieces of ice are also entropic objects. Think about your ice cubes in a freezer: they shrink over time, that is called sublimation. Consequently, the lifespan of an ice core is only about a hundred years. Of course, one could go back to the glacier or ice sheet and potentially extract another core, but it will be a different one and in some cases the glacier may have already completely vanished. Thus, there is a finite temporality to the ice core, even if it hasn't already been cut up, crushed, melted, and subjected to various analyses. The video also discusses the fact that air is always younger than the ice itself as the air circulates freely amongst snow crystals until it is finally sealed off by the weight of successive generations of snow fall. So, we have a multiplicity of temporalities in the same set of ice core samples. There is also a key lesson that one has to learn when working with an ice core: you can't ever accidentally flip the sample on its head (which is around one meter in length and forms part of a multi-kilometer core) because you would invert its temporal registers as well as the data it contains, which is crucial for building the global climate model. Alison explains this in one scene in the video. So, you see, there are many conditions of temporality that are at stake when working with the cores themselves.

Charlotte: Since you mentioned temporal glitches that become evident, ice cores appear as epistemic objects that make legible social, political, and technological history. As we touched on the issue of historicity and different time scales already, could you expand on your approach and observations regarding the making of history in relation to the material objects and infrastructures that may support it?

Susan: This condition has become increasingly interesting for me in terms of thinking about the question of history in relationship to ice cores. Earth doesn't have a history per se. History is a cultural construct. Things have gone on in the past, but the Earth itself, that is to say the planet, doesn't have a conception of its own history, but rather we could say that materials like ice cores and the ways that they are studied allow us to make a kind of retroactive claim, or they allow us to make the claim that Earth has a history. I am interested in the ways in which materials enable these kinds of epistemic moves to be made. While the natural world doesn't have history, the intercession of different technical and investigative probes enables us to narrate the material world and make claims with those materials, such that we can say that ice cores are one of the means by which we can make the very provocative claim that the Earth has a history. It is a means for making that cultural move. And to me, this kind of epistemic transformation is enabled by ice cores that transform this place that we live on into a subject with a history and a proper name. And that proper name is Planet Earth.

Throughout the project *Material Witness*, I was trying to look at the ways in which materials enable certain epistemic transformations to take place and to de-naturalize the ways in which we position ourselves with respect to the ancient climactic histories of the planet. There is a fantastic text[5] that looks at the invention of stratigraphy as enabling a conception of historical change through the spatial typology of layered events. With such a diagram in place, one can start to go back in time and address different historical layers and attribute cultural understandings to the material changes evidenced or evinced by such layered entities.[6]

Jakob: Thank you for bringing up your notion of material witness again, as it strongly informed the questions about material infrastructures that may bear witness to environmental dynamics. What interested us, among others things, is the question of how infrastructures themselves can become seismographs and archives of environmental dynamics. That implies that human-made structures can be understood as a sensitive network, since they are rather fragile to changing natural or social environments. It opens up a tension between a kind of perfectionist, seamless or idealistic envisioning of infrastructures on the one hand – be they cooling systems, roads, or storage facilities – and the constant care and maintenance work in order to keep the systems and their functionality working on the other. As is discussed in your video, the infrastructures and technologies that preserve the icy data are themselves subject to scientific and political dynamics, financing questions, and ageing technologies. Or to frame it differently: How did you experience the tensions between the site-specific interaction and practices and possible (political/societal) demands or imaginaries regarding infrastructural elements?

Susan: This is a crucial question, especially in the Canadian context. Precisely for the reason that the Canadian ice cores

---

5   Here Susan is referring to David Sepkoski's 2017 article "The Earth as Archive: Contingency, Narrative, and the History of Life."

6   Susan is referring, among other things, to scholarly works by Dipesh Chakrabarty (2009), Isabel Stengers (2015), and Quentin Meillassoux's concept of the "arche-fossil" (2014, 10).

were largely extracted from the Canadian high Arctic in the 1970s, when there was a very active research program in place. But due to shifting research priorities, especially under the conservative Harper government from 2006 to 2015, research directions and priorities in Canada shifted. The budget for maintaining the collection of Arctic cores was completely slashed and the government was literally on the verge of unplugging the freezer in Ottawa where they were stored and letting all the ice melt in a parking lot. Martin Sharp, an Earth and atmospheric scientist at the University of Alberta, put together the funds to both move the collection to Edmonton and build a purpose-built ice core archive, where they could be securely stored, especially in light of the fact that no active coring has taken place in Canada and in the Arctic for a long time now. The future of the archive was entirely contingent on finding the funding resources to keep the cores at -25/-30 Celsius. But as I mentioned before, the triple malfunction of the freezer shows how precarious these infrastructures and materialities really are.

Put pragmatically, the only reason that the cores still exist today is because there was a scientific will to keep the archival infrastructure operational, including its ongoing upkeep and long-term maintenance. A somewhat related point, which is not something that is addressed in the *Ice Core* film directly, emerged out of a really interesting interview I conducted with the nuclear physicist John Rowat in 2016, who works for the International Atomic Energy Agency. We were discussing various proposals for the geological storage of radioactive contaminants, and he made a rather telling point: We need to live in proximity to contaminants, we need to live in proximity to the disaster zone. His impression was that taking environmental contaminants such as radioactive waste and depositing it somewhere in Finland, for example in Onkalo, was not sustainable. If we actually want to make sure that there is ongoing preservation, care, and maintenance of these techno-infrastructures, especially those dealing with hazardous waste, they need to be embedded into the social, cultural fabric of communities. We need to live in proximity to them. That is the only way that mitigating disasters and risks might actually be guaranteed. If we think we can just move them out of sight and out of mind, eventually something is going to happen. They are going to be neglected. For me that was an interesting way to rethink a whole set of strategies around these disposal sites. If we want to manage these records of anthropogenic disaster, it is necessary to develop relationships of critical proximity. When you first think about it, it might seem slightly counter-intuitive, but I tend to agree that if we want to think about ongoing maintenance, repair, as well as the security and stability of these infrastructures, they really need to be part of our everyday lives. So once again, we need to focus on the minor dramas of the everyday, to avoid the major drama of another nuclear event. But I take the point that the necessity for developing relationships of critical proximity is really the only way that we can ensure the long-term care and preservation of some of these dangerous sites.

Charlotte: *Ice Cores* is part of a larger project extending over different media, time, and places as well as actors and (working) networks; all of this is held together by the question of what you call a politics of cold, directing the focus on the aesthetic and epistemic power of ice and the political and ethical dimensions it opens. We would like to return to the broader context of the video: What has happened since it was finished? What are you working on currently and what future undertakings are ahead of you? And as we have talked a lot about methodologies in and for artistic research: How has your practice changed during this project and how do you shift between the various methodological approaches and topics that you engage with?

Susan: The final part of the *Learning from Ice* project is an acoustic mapping project called *Siku Sense* that will take place in Nunavut. It has been postponed due to Covid but will be the next project after my current field work in Svalbard, which begins this coming weekend. There I'll be working on a community satellite project and podcast series that is largely focused on environmental transmissions and involves interviewing different people, as well as going to different sites, such as the *Kjell Henriksen Observatory* and *SvalSat*, which is the world's biggest satellite ground station. We will also travel by snowmobile to Isford Radio, which is a defunct radio station about 100 kilometers away on the coast. There are many technical infrastructures that converge on Svalbard and so I'm hoping to try and capture a sense of this transmissional condition rather than its strictly eco-touristic qualities. I suppose I will be moving away from a direct engagement with ice, but continuing to work within a cryospheric context.

As a final note, in regard to the work that I have been doing in *Learning from Ice* as well as with the Svalbard-project, I was confronted with environments that I knew were very saturated with politics, that weren't necessarily available to me in the visual field. Consequently, I decided to make a series of videos called *Cold Cases* in collaboration with Forensic Architecture[7] that focus on human right violations inflicted on bodies by

7 Forensic Architecture is an interdisciplinary research agency established in 2010 by the architect and theorist Eyal Weizman together with a group of fellow architects, artists, filmmakers, journalists, scientists, and lawyers. The agency produces "evidence files" including "building survey, models, animations, video analyses, and interactive cartographies" and presents them in political and juridical forums such as international courts, truth commissions, citizen tribunals, or human rights and environmental reports. See Weizman (2017, 9) and https://forensic-architecture.org (accessed June 20, 2022).

means of cold temperatures. These are videos in which the political dimensions of environments are very explicit.[8] So in my continuous artistic research practice one project formulates the demand to do something differently in the next and respond to open questions. *Cold Cases* is not field-based but entirely archival and perhaps could be considered didactic. It lacks the poetic sensibility that the other works have, by necessity. The insight into the condition of temperature and its instrumentalization came to me while working on the *Ice Cores* documentary when I started to think about the production of artificial cold in the context of filming the technology and infrastructure that is required for keeping the ice core archive in a state of deep freeze. One project plants a seed that may eventually at some later date make its way into something else…

8 Susan is referring here to her work *Cold Cases* (2021-2022).

Chakrabarty, Dipesh. 2009. "The Climate of History: Four Theses." *Critical Inquiry* 35 (2): 197–222.

Deleuze, Gilles. 2004. "The Method of Dramatization." In *Desert Islands and Other Texts 1953-1974*, edited by David Lapoujade, translated by Michael Taormina, 94–116. Cambridge, MA: Semiotext(e).

Deleuze, Gilles. 2006. "Making Inaudible Forces Audible." In *Two Regimes of Madness: Texts and Interviews 1975-1995,* edited by David Lapoujade, 156–60. Cambridge, MA: Semiotext(e).

Derworiz, Colette. 2017 "Unique Canadian Ice Core Collection Suffers Catastrophic Meltdown." *Science*. Accessed June 20, 2022. https://science.org/content/article/unique-canadian-ice-core-collection-suffers-catastrophic-meltdown.

Haraway, Donna J. 2016. *Staying with the Trouble: Making Kin in the Chthulucene*. Durham, NC/London: Duke University Press.

Holert, Tom. 2020. *Knowledge beside Itself: Contemporary Art's Epistemic Politics*. Berlin: Sternberg Press.

Latour, Bruno. 1999. *Pandora's Hope: Essays on the Reality of Science Studies*. Cambridge, MA: Harvard University Press.

Meillassoux, Quentin. 2014. *After Finitude: An Essay on the Necessity of Contingency*. London: Bloomsbury Academic.

Morton, Timothy. 2013. *Hyperobjects: Philosophy and Ecology after the End of the World*. Minneapolis, MN: University of Minnesota Press.

Rheinberger, Hans-Jörg. 1997. *Toward a History of Epistemic Things: Synthesizing Proteins in the Test Tube*. Stanford, CA: Stanford University Press.

Schuppli, Susan. 2020. *Material Witness: Media, Forensics, Evidence*. Cambridge, MA: MIT Press.

Sepkoski, David. 2017. "The Earth as Archive: Contingency, Narrative, and the History of Life." In *Science in the Archives: Pasts, Presents, Futures*, edited by Lorraine Daston, 53–83. Chicago, IL: University of Chicago Press.

Stengers, Isabelle. 2015. *In Catastrophic Times: Resisting the Coming Barbarism*. Translated by Andrew Goffey. London: Open Humanities Press.

Weizman, Eyal. 2017. *Forensic Architecture: Violence at the Threshold of Detectability*. Brooklyn, NY: Zone Books.

ESSAY

Infrastructures in Time and Anthropogenic Climate Change

Gabriele Schabacher

Infrastructures are material traces of climate change in a threefold sense. They are major contributors to climate change, they represent forms of coping with and combating climate change (more sustainable energy or transport systems), and they economically affirm and exploit it. To understand these interrelationships, this paper takes a closer look at the temporal constitution of infrastructures. It discusses the relationship between infrastructure and collapse as a form of their fundamental processuality, and distinguishes four ways in which infrastructures can be said to be "in time": their everyday fragility, their overlapping lifetimes, their status as remnants and ruins, and their relevance in the horizon of the Anthropocene. The example of Arctic shipping is discussed to show how climate change and the resulting navigability of the Arctic region are fundamentally altering the global geopolitical network of supply and exchange relationships.

Keywords: Infrastructure, Climate Change, Anthropocene, Temporality, Disruption, Ruin, Lifetimes, Care, Arctic Shipping

63

1   The research literature on anthropogenic climate change is extraordinarily extensive. In particular, the concept of the Anthropocene has been widely discussed in this context. Initially informed by the natural sciences (Crutzen 2002; Will et al. 2011), it then became central to the humanities as well (Chakrabarty 2009; Horn and Bergthaller 2019). For critiques of the term, especially in light of its implicit assumptions and exclusions, see, for example, Harraway 2015; Moore 2017; Yusoff 2018. On the relationship of infrastructure and environment specifically, see Hetherington 2019. For further literature, see the references in section 2.

Infrastructures play an important role with regard to anthropogenic climate change.[1] Heuristically, at least three respects can be distinguished in which they do so. For infrastructures can be considered equally as causes, handlings, and profiteers of climate change. Insofar as the establishment of infrastructures has been linked to industrialization and urbanization since the beginning of the nineteenth century, for whose success the use of fossil energies was primarily responsible, they must first be seen as the cause of climate crisis. Second, they provide opportunities for dealing with climate change, whether in the form of scientific methods or through the development of new climate-friendly technologies. And third, infrastructures can also be seen as the winners of climate change, specifically calculating with the consequences of it. To better understand the different relations between infrastructures and anthropogenic climate change, this paper proposes to focus on the temporal dimension of infrastructures. For not only is anthropogenic climate change a temporal phenomenon, this applies equally to the infrastructures that interact with it.

Low water levels of the Rhine and other rivers, uncontrollable forest fires in Spain and Portugal, the faster melting of alpine glaciers and resulting landslides (for example in the Marmolata massif), these are only some of the "records of disasters", as this volume calls them, that characterized the European summer of 2022. But we can also look back to 2021 and think, for instance, of the flooding in the Ahr valley in Rhineland-Palatinate, the heat waves in North America, the hurricane season or the Corona pandemic, for which the crossing of the animal-human boundary (zoonosis) as a result of the destruction of natural habitats as well as excessive animal use is being discussed as a possible cause – in all these cases we receive pictures and videos, reports from eyewitnesses, scientific data and problem analyses of the ecological crisis events in question. Here, infrastructures are involved in the sense of processing telecommunication (transmission of data) or storage media providing such records. These records, in turn, are assessed scientifically, for example, in the context of attribution research (Otto 2020), which statistically evaluates the relative contributions of various causal factors to climate change, paying particular attention to the relationship between anthropogenic climate change and extreme weather events. But not only the images and reports are records of disaster; in a certain sense, the destroyed bridges, flooded roads, burned houses themselves must be considered to be such records, namely as material traces of climate change.

In this context, the concept of "material witness" as developed by Susan Schuppli is relevant. This term, in its operative sense, as opposed to its legal usage (a person "*pertinent*" to the outcome of a lawsuit), emphasizes the testimonial capacity of nonhuman actors, quite literally in the sense of "material *as* witness" (2020, 10), which provides traces *of* and *to* a history of political violence. Materials, however, are not witnesses per se. They only become such "when the complex histories interwoven in the objects are unfolded […] and put up for public consideration and discussion" (2020, 18), lending relevance to the conditions and procedures that turn such eventful materials into testimonies (2020, 20). Such a perspective on the testimonial quality of matter, however, is not self-evident. Only an interest in the mediality of personal witnesses and the transmission of knowledge carried out by them brings to the fore the ambivalence between personalization (the authentic witness) and depersonalization (the witness as a 'neutral' recording device) associated with this process (Krämer 2015, 152). It is then above all the "*forensic turn*" (Däumer, Kalisky and Schlie 2017, 14), exemplified, along with Schuppli, by the work of the research collective Forensic Architecture in particular, which focuses on the potential of objects and findings to bear witness to events and experiences, establishing a close connection between media and forensics by means of the concept of the trace (Rothöhler 2021).

What do we gain by applying the concept of material witnessing to the connection between infrastructures and climate change? Seeing infrastructures as material witnesses of anthropogenic climate change, that is, to understand them themselves as records (inscriptions) of ecological disaster, thus means considering them not only as transmission networks that make climate change traceable. Rather, the infrastructures of energy, transport, and production represent essential causal factors for the emergence of anthropogenic climate change. At the same time, they are substantially involved in reshaping existing conditions, with two diametrically opposed tendencies: for the "good" (establishing sustainable forms of transport, production, energy supply, etc.) and for the "bad" (economic exploitation of the very opportunities created by anthropogenic climate change, which further accelerates it). From this perspective, infrastructures can be understood as active mediators of climate change. We will see in the following how and at which levels this understanding is related to the specific temporality and materiality of infrastructures.

The argument will unfold in four steps. At first, I will discuss the connection between infrastructures (especially "critical infrastructures") and breakdown and address its epistemological relevance. In the next section, I will outline four different ways in which one can speak of "infrastructures in time," namely, their everyday fragility, their aging (not their obsolescence), their status as leftovers after they are no longer in use, and finally their geo-temporal dimension with reference to the Anthropocene. The temporality of infrastructures in the horizon of the Anthropocene is unfolded in more detail in the third section with reference to the recent example of Arctic shipping. I will show how economic actors are building a new shipping infrastructure in deliberate preparation for the fact that anthropogenic climate change will have intensified to the point that the Northwest and Northeast Passages will be navigable without ice by 2040. A brief conclusion will summarize the main arguments and provide an outlook.

Infrastructures and Breakdown

What is the significance of disasters and accidents for infrastructures? If we take a look at the history of railroad development in the nineteenth century, for example, we are first struck by the immense frequency of devastating accidents (derailments, head-on collisions, bridge collapses, etc.), especially in the first decades (Aldrich 2006). Only towards the end of the nineteenth century does the severity and frequency of accidents decrease. In between lies what I have elsewhere called "infrastructural learning" (Schabacher 2022, 175; 2019, 194), which underscores the epistemic importance of accidents and disasters for understanding technical processes and events (Kassung 2009). This is because such disruptions allow infrastructures to emerge from their black-box state; in a sense, they disintegrate again into individual actors (*mediators*) that are coordinated in the infrastructural state (*intermediaries*) (Latour 1996, 176f.). Thus, functional relationships of infrastructures can be analyzed and subsequently changed; for example, derailments draw attention to how track beds must be fixed to withstand various weather conditions, or how railroad crossings must be secured to prevent people from being run over. The state of being deblackboxed is also conceptualized in Science and Technology Studies as the visibility of infrastructures; Susan Leigh Star and Karen Ruhleder, for example, speak of infrastructures becoming "visible upon breakdown" (Star amd Ruhleder 1996, 113). What is meant is the fact that they come to the forefront of attention in the face of disruption (not that the actors and agents mentioned are not actually visible), that is, they become explicit, "bulky," and uncomfortable in their materiality and non-functioning. I use the term disruption here in a broad sense in terms of media theory (Schüttpelz 2002; Neubert 2012), referring to disruptive phenomena in the broadest sense, ranging from technical defects to system accidents (Perrow 1984) to natural disasters and terrorist attacks, and including the cultural imaginaries and anxieties that accompany them (Horn 2016; Koch, Nanz, and Pause 2018).

As a present example, the war in Ukraine makes abundantly clear that infrastructures first and foremost have the task of providing what is known as "services of general interest" (German: *Daseinsvorsorge*): they supply us with what we need to live – energy, water, food, but also communications, cultural and transport facilities.[2] And because this function is essential, they are referred to as critical infrastructures (Rinaldi, Peerenboom and Kelly 2001; Engels 2018). If they fail, this has serious consequences: Europe no longer receives gas; the Middle East no longer receives wheat. The Ukraine war has put the spotlight on the otherwise inconspicuous axes of global supply and exchange relationships. Pipelines, ports, power plants, and railroads are becoming visible in their regulating function of guaranteeing or preventing access to certain resources.[3] Infrastructures are thus always threatened, they represent vulnerable points of communities and states and are thus possible targets of attacks.

But infrastructures are not only fragile when attacked in times of war. Already in the early 2000s, Paul Virilio curated an exhibition explicitly dedicated to questions of the accident. Titled *Ce qui arrive,* it was dedicated to the exposition (read: making visible) of accidents to analyze what threats the modern world faces (2002). Virilio was thinking of the deforestation in the Amazon region, meteorite impacts, the effects of radioactivity (atomic bomb/atomic power), chemical accidents, oil tanker accidents, airplane crashes, 9/11, wars, and natural disasters. Frequently, the illustrations center around the disastrous impact on urban infrastructures. For example, we see roads and houses destroyed by earthquakes (→1), flooded motorways, electric poles bent by ice loads (2002, 10–20, 34, 35).

One of the central insights of Virilio's accident theory is that every technology generates its own accident (2007, 10). While Virilio focuses on the fortunes of the respective vehicles (the shipwreck, the derailment, the pileup), I want to emphasize the infrastructural dimension of such accidents and disruptions. For when the Ever Given is stranded in the Suez Canal for six days (→2), this is essentially not a singular local occurrence. Rather it is an event of global scope that makes logistical trade linkages palpable and shows that the insight Latour formulated for the railroad network applies even more in this case: a global network is local at each of its points (Latour 1993, 171).

2   This concept, coined in 1938 by the constitutional lawyer Ernst Forsthoff, assumes that man exchanges the individual securing of livelihood for a spatial expansion of his living relations. In this way, however, he becomes fundamentally dependent on what the state can provide (Forsthoff 1938).

3   For example, the well-developed Ukrainian railroad system was targeted by Russian attacks because it is logistically crucial for transporting weapons, aid, and supplies (Latschan 2022).

If the Ever Given is stuck or the port of Shanghai cannot handle goods (→ 3), as was the case during the two-month Covid lockdown in spring 2022, this immediately has noticeable effects everywhere. Accidents and disasters thus make us aware of infrastructures insofar as they show what we assume (and expect) as their normal functioning.

But focusing on the catastrophic states of infrastructures is not without problems. For it implicitly assumes that a calm, balanced, and ultimately accident-free normal state exists on the flip side of catastrophic situations (Graham/Thrift 2007, 9f.). However, closer examination of concrete working environments of large-scale technical systems (Potthast 2008; Wynne 1988), but also intercultural studies (Larkin 2008) have unmasked this idea of a supposedly "calm" normal operation as a specifically Western illusion that unquestioningly presupposes certain properties of technology. Now this does not at all mean that a more unsettled normal operation can only be found in the Global South, but rather that the Western notion of technical normal operation has long prevented us from even taking a closer look at the supposedly stable state of technology and infrastructures. In addition, catastrophes often do not take the form of major events alone. Instead – and this is particularly relevant with regard to climate change – they consist of a large number of small changes, none of which is serious in itself, but which build up in such a way that at a *tipping point* (Gladwell 2000; Horn 2016, 148–56) they catalytically set in motion an irreversible catastrophic development.

2   Ever given stuck in the Suez Canal, March 23, 2021 (Source: Detail from a satellite image
     by Pleiades, Airbus, © CNES 2021, Distribution Airbus DS. Accessed August 23, 2022.
     https://intelligence-airbusds.com/en/5751-image-gallery-details?img=65560#.YwTAQE9CTmg)

3   Traffic jam off Shanghai, April 28, 2022. Symbols: cargo ships (green), tankers (red), anchored/
     moored (circles), on the move (triangles) (Source: Chart. "Shanghai Ship Jam Spells Out
     Supply Chain Trouble". *Statista.com*. April 28, 2022. Accessed August 23, 2022.
     https://statista.com/chart/27343/container-ship-backlog-off-shanghai-port/)

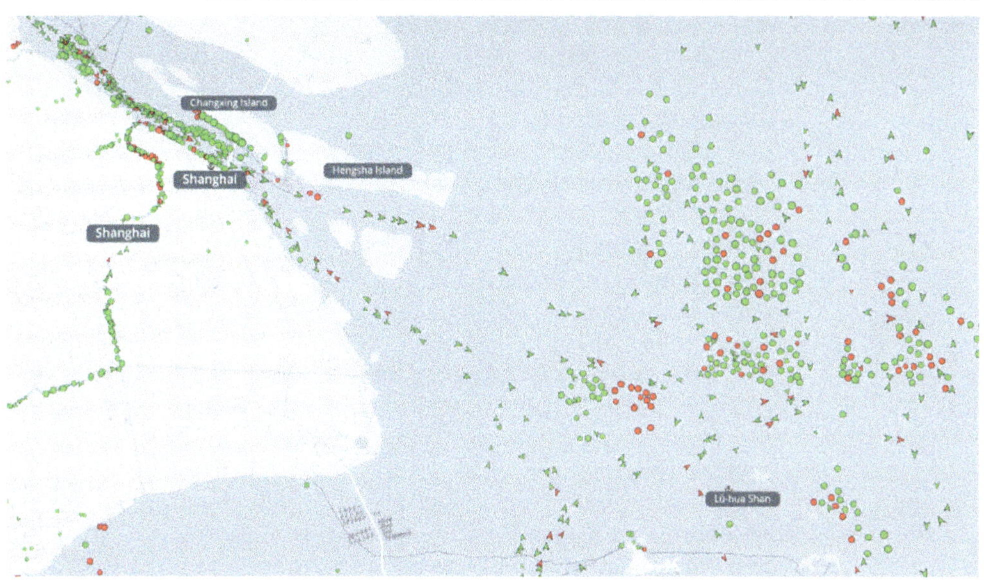

Beyond catastrophes, however, the "normal" functioning of infrastructures is already more susceptible to disruption than is generally assumed. It therefore makes sense, as I will elaborate below, to assume a fundamentally precarious relationship between fragility and stability for infrastructures, that is, to reformulate their materiality and organization as a temporal issue.

Temporal Regimes of Infrastructures
Infrastructures are indeed "in time" in a specific way. Heuristically, (at least) four different temporal regimes can be distinguished: first, the already mentioned everyday fragility of infrastructures; second, the phenomenon of aging infrastructures, where a kind of overlapping of temporal layers occurs; third, the temporal constitution of infrastructures when they are no longer in use and we encounter them as remnants; and fourth, finally, their temporality in geological terms related to the Anthropocene debate.

Processuality of Infrastructures
To understand the precarious relationship between fragility and stability more precisely, it is important to focus on two opposing processes. For on the one hand, infrastructures are determined by processes whose goal is to stabilize fragile states. On the other hand, however, supposedly stable or, better, stabilized states are always destabilized again. I refer to these two processes as "infrastructure work," as the work *on* and *of* infrastructures (Schabacher 2022, 20–1). What is important here is the following paradox. The processes of stabilizing infrastructures involve, for instance, activities of maintenance, repair, cleaning, that is, in the broadest sense, forms of care and concern that take place recurrently over a long period of time to ensure their functioning. Such repairs after minor or major disruptions, however, are always accompanied by changes – new parts are connected to old parts, different people treat systems and technologies in different ways, new regulations require changed ways of handling them, etc. Thus, the activities aimed at stabilization always have transformative effects whereby they contribute to the transformation of infrastructures. I understand this temporal quality as the processuality of infrastructures (Schabacher 2022, 133).

The fact that the fragility of infrastructures also has to do with climatic factors is part of the everyday knowledge of the modern age. Every year in spring, asphalt road surfaces that have been cracked by winter frost have to be repaired. In the fall, squares, sidewalks, and other traffic routes must be cleaned of fallen leaves, after heavy rains slopes must be resurfaced and filled, and iron elements prone to rust must be repainted

regularly. In addition, of course, there are other forms of disruption, such as vandalism, wear and tear of components, etc. Thus, "material fragility" (Denis and Pontille 2015, 341) characterizes all artifacts and infrastructures. Only when this vulnerability is taken into account can order and stability be established. In the maintenance of the wayfinding system of the Paris subway, for example, the respective technicians have to regularly repair damage, wear and tear, and mold on the signboards, but also update information and make adjustments related to the standardization policy (Denis and Pontille 2015,

355). In doing so, their work cannot be normalized, as part of their job is to cope with very heterogeneous environments and situational problems. In contrast to the subway users, who mainly perceive the standardization of the signage, for the maintenance staff the signboards exist in a fragile and vulnerable state. Repair and maintenance are thus not marginal activities; rather, they represent the heart of modern economies and societies, their "engine room" (Graham and Thrift 2007, 19). And this is the case in economic terms as well, because repair and maintenance activities represent a large part of economic activity (many jobs), even if this is often not considered (Graham and Thrift 2007, 7). For even if the fragility of infrastructures is an economically relevant factor, the activities directed at them are themselves often comparatively invisible (Star/Strauss 1989; Illich 1981). This is because repair and maintenance work belongs to the large field of care work (Degeling and Haffke 2021; Puig de la Bellacasa 2017), which is no longer profitable in the horizon of industrially produced mass and disposable products. It is especially the environmental movement that make cultural techniques of care (Schabacher 2020) relevant again. The relative invisibility of care work also has to do with the fact that it is often not paid or paid less (domestic work and foster care) and partly carried out by less recognized groups of people. It is therefore always about the "politics of repair" (Graham and Thrift 2007, 18) – who repairs, how this is paid for, and whether repair knowledge is provided or prevented.

What happens when repair and maintenance work is not carried out can be illustrated by a look at the situation of U.S. infrastructures. For the failure to make necessary repairs leads to costs rising year by year as problems continue to mount. Since 1998 the American Society of Civil Engineers (ASCE), a professional association of civil engineers concerned with planning, designing, constructing, and operating the built environment, has been assessing the condition of U.S. infrastructures every four years, using the format of an A to F school report card. According to the 2021 infrastructure report card (→ 4) the "infrastructure investment gap," that is, the costs that would be due to repair the ailing infrastructures (read: reach grade B), is put at about 2.59 trillion U.S. dollars (ASCE 2021, 5).

If appropriate investments are not made now, it is projected that by 2039 the funding gap would already be about $10 trillion, costing each U.S. household the equivalent of $3,300 a year or $63 a week (ASCE 2021). Although the report acknowledges that "some incremental progress" (ASCE 2021, 2) has been made, in long-term perspective the investment gap still grows (ASCE 2021, 5). While the condition of bridges, drinking water, and energy, for example, has improved minimally since 2017, with the grade point average (G.P.A.) for all 17 categories assessed rising from D+ to an average grade of C-, this is still a long way from the targeted B.[4] Of the 617,000 bridges, for instance, 42 per cent are at least 50 years old and over 46,000 are in very poor condition, yet these bridges are crossed 178 million times per day. If the current investment rate were to be maintained, it would take until 2071 to carry out all the necessary repairs, not including further deterioration caused, for example, by extreme weather events (flooding, washouts, storm damage), to which ailing bridges are particularly susceptible (ASCE 2021, 19 and 23). So, unlike consumer goods, which according to the product life cycle calculated for them are to be discarded at the end of their (short) lives and replaced by new goods (Stark 2015),[5] this is not the case with large-scale infrastructures. Since the investment costs are very high, they are not taken out of service in the event of a malfunction but must be continuously repaired and kept running.[6] This is also the reason why the ASCE, in addition to sufficient funding, recommends preventive maintenance programs as solution strategies (ASCE 2021).[7]

Life Age Stratifications
A second perspective on infrastructures in time concerns the fact that they themselves age. Unlike the first case, this is not a matter of materials becoming porous or signs yellowing that need to be replaced or repaired to ensure the functioning of the infrastructure in question. Rather, in this case the infrastructure is functioning smoothly, but its components stem from different ages. In the case of very long-lived and complex infrastructures, the resulting temporal layering is particularly noticeable.

For example, the space mission to explore Saturn and its moons, conducted by NASA in collaboration with the European Space Agency (ESA) and the Italian Space Agency (ASI), lasted about 35 years. Accordingly, not only the spacecraft itself, but also the technical infrastructure that supported the operation and maintenance of this mission in a laboratory on the ground had to be operated for a correspondingly long time. The space craft was planned and constructed since 1982, launched in 1997, reached Saturn in 2004 and began collecting data. In 2010 it was extended for a final phase till 2017. The system thus consisted of "multiple lifetimes of different parts of the system – hardware, software, code, organizational processes, programming languages, institutions, careers – all of which are entangled and are aging or obsolescing at different

4 For an overview of the overall development in the various categories, see ASCE 2021, 167.

5 Turned positive, this is called *circular economy* in the sense of the *cradle to cradle* principle (McDonough and Braungart 2002; Borrion, Black, and Mwabonje 2021); turned negative, it appears as planned obsolescence (Slade 2006).

6 Such cascades of use of things familiar from the pre-modern economy of scarcity (Stöger 2015) can be found today as the reuse of bicycles, cell phones, computers and second-hand clothing in West and East Africa (Hahn 2018; Malefakis 2018).

7 The situation is quite similar to that of Deutsche Bahn. Here, too, repairs are urgently due. In 2022 alone, 13.6 billion are to be spent on renovating the ailing rail infrastructure (1,800 kilometers of tracks, 2,000 switches, 140 bridges, and 800 stations) and 4,800 new jobs are to be created for this purpose (Deutsche Bahn 2022). For this reason, the German federal government and Deutsche Bahn have already agreed on a package of measures for 2020 (BMVI 2020), according to which around 86 billion euros will be invested in modernization by 2030.

rates" (Cohn 2016, 1513). Maintaining the functionality of such a space probe thus meant that a system of several-decades-old technology and software must be kept running by people who in turn must know to handle this 'old' technology. In this case, the maintenance technicians aged with the technology they supported: "Infrastructural decay is a process that emerges through the ways that different parts of the system, aging at different rates are entangled with each other. What decays or ages are the relations across multiple parts of the infrastructure and among people, the organization, and its technologies" (Cohn 2016, 1519). In a similar way, old machines (in museums, for example) can only be kept running (for demonstration purposes, let's say) if there are still people around who know how to operate them.

Such temporal stratifications of life ages are very often also found in the infrastructures of public administration. Unlike in a high-tech company (and even here this applies only with restrictions), public institutions increasingly have devices of different ages (some of them drastically outdated) alongside each other (PCs, copiers, printers, telephones, etc.). In addition, there are people of different ages who are correspondingly adapted to newer or older technologies; likewise, manuals, routines, legal regulations, and forms of organization often originate from different times. One only has to think of the excessive demands made on the health authorities at the beginning of the Corona crisis, when the need to track contacts digitally came up against a process handling system that was still largely oriented toward paper and fax (Kinkartz 2020). In each of these cases, 'keeping it functional' means: dealing with the imponderabilities of the specific local circumstances, including variously aged machines, regulations, and people, and balancing them so that the desired processes work to some degree. In this respect, then, infrastructures are in time in the sense of the heterogeneous ages of things, people, regulations, and processes that are embedded and intertwined within them.

Infrastructure Remnants
But infrastructures are also "in time" in a third respect. Unlike products that decompose or get recycled, infrastructures are often characterized by a high degree of resistance, which can also be understood as their "obduracy-in-obsolescence" (Cairns and Jacobs 2014, 111). What is meant is the fact that they remain marked as remnants even in the state of abandonment (for a more detailed analysis Schabacher 2018). What can generally be stated for the space-time relationship of building ruins therefore also applies to abandoned infrastructures: they are "regularly out of time [...] but still very

much in place" (Cairns and Jacobs 2014, 58). This is because, unlike infrastructures in operation, which tend to fade into the background as a taken-for-granted part of routines of action, abandoned infrastructures are still there, even when they are no longer in use (→ 5).

Concerning the nostalgia or *ruin porn* (Lyons 2018; Whitehouse 2018) that is inspired by these abandoned infrastructures, it can be shown how, in a way, they become landscape again. For we often find photographic representations of built structures that are reconquered by nature, which thus reside in a peculiar intermediate "zombie" status between nature and culture (Schabacher 2018, 129). They function as "material witnesses" of historical conditions, be it in an economic sense (think of former industrial sites),[8] be it in an imperial context as lasting traces of colonial structures of governance (*ruins of empire*) that have lasting effects on the present (Gordillo 2014; Stoler 2016), or be it as signs of military conflicts (*ruins of wars*) (Virilio 1994).

8   Detroit has become iconic for this (Levine and Moore 2010; Apel 2015).

This applies not only to the material side of infrastructures, but equally to their social, cultural, and organizational aspects. The *obduracy* of infrastructures can thus be understood as their resistance to change, which is expressed both in the "fixed" views about them, the embeddedness of their components in the environmental space, and in the traditions persisting through them (Hommels 2008, 21–39). One could say that these aspects become even stronger when the infrastructure in question is no longer used. Its very existence marks limitations of people's life realities, but also refers to the historical and affective ruptures that accompany such debris (Gordillo 2014). Ann Laura Stoler addresses these connections as the "duress" (2016, 7) of imperial leftovers, understood in the threefold sense of their hardness or constraint, durability, and duration which she also frames as the "colonial *presence*" (2016, 33) of imperial debris. Her question is how people "live *with* and *in* ruins" (2016, 353) in order to address the toxic effects of imperial remains on actual living realities. Particularly relevant are the ecological legacies of empire, which express a form of "environmental racism" (2016, 351), for instance when it comes to the unequal distribution of pollution and waste disposal with regard to impoverished population groups (Carruthers 2008; Nixon 2011): "Imperial ruins are [...] *racialized markers on a global scale*" (Stoler 2016, 353). The reading proposed for the term "ruin" is crucial here. For the focus is not solely on the condition of a thing, but rather also on the process of "ruination" that affects it: "Ruination is an *act* perpetrated, a *condition* to which one is subject, and a *cause* of loss" (Stoler 2016, 350). With reference to the relation between *matter* and *mattering* (Cairns and Jacobs 2014, 49; Thompson 1979), it can therefore be emphasized, with reference to Stoler, that in the case of abandoned infrastructures not only the material remnants are relevant, but also their respective positioning and valuations within current political discourses.

Infrastructures in the Anthropocene
The fourth and last respect in which I want to discuss the temporality of infrastructures relates to the horizon of the Anthropocene. As with the discussion of infrastructure ruins in the previous section, this also concerns effects of infrastructures, but now on a different scale. For now, it is the planetary dimension of the geological implications of infrastructures that is at issue, which changes the relations of man and environments in long-lasting ways.

This situation has been referred to as "anthroturbation" (Zalasiewicz, Waters, and Williams 2014), as the disturbance of the Earth by human activity. The term is derived from the geoscientific term "bioturbation," which describes fossil traces, such as burrows and feeding tracks, that invertebrates (such as worms and clams) left in rocks as early as the Cambrian period, 600 million years ago. Applied to humans, it is also a matter of tracing their feeding tracks and burrows, so to say. And these permanent traces are the infrastructures created by humans, which massively transform our planet at the latest

9   As mentioned at the outset, however, speaking of "the Anthropocene" has certain biases. For both questions of causation and how it affects us are not equally distributed across all of humanity (Yusoff 2018). A term like *capitalocene* takes this unequal distribution into account (Moore 2016).

with the Industrial Revolution and have lasting (and often irreversible) effects on the geography of the earth.[9] This affects three levels (Zalasiewicz, Waters, and Williams 2014, 4–5): Anthroturbation changes the Earth's *surface* by engineering landscapes, soils, oceans, and the atmosphere (human constructions, excavations, and other interventions in urban and agricultural environments). It alters *subsurface* layers through structures built at shallow depths, such as systems of energy supply, sewerage, and transportation like subway urban networks, subways, and tunnels. And it alters the earth through *deep anthroturbation* such as mining and drilling in particular.

Against this backdrop, different actors and activities are held responsible as prime movers and drivers of the Anthropocene. The concept of the *plantationocene*, for example, emphasizes the extensive conversion of farmland and forests into enclosed plantations through slave labor (Haraway 2015); the *oleocene* emphasizes the general importance of fossil fuels and the infrastructures of the oil drilling industry; and the *anthrobscene* refers to the "obscene" economics of all materials necessary to produce the contemporary media world (Parikka 2014). Moreover, the global disposal of waste which generates nuclear waste repositories as well as satellite debris orbiting the Earth (Parks 2013; Damjanow 2017; Clormann and Klimburrg-Witjes 2022), the Great Pacific Garbage Patch (Vehlken 2020; Reichle 2021), should also be mentioned here.

As I outlined at the beginning, three respects can be analytically distinguished in which infrastructures are related to the Anthropocene. In the anthroturbation phenomenon just discussed, infrastructures turn out to be primary causes and "material witnesses" of climate change in the Anthropocene. In a second respect, however, they can also be encountered as forces and structures responding to climate change. Here, too, a connection between infrastructures and the Anthropocene emerges, but now insofar as they are transformations and treatments of existing constellations that seek to minimize the effects of climate change: "new" infrastructures, so to speak, that treat "old" infrastructures. We might think, for example, of the transformation of energy production, that is, the closure of lignite mining sites in favor of decentralized, renewable forms of energy (wind farms, solar power plants). We might also think of the transformation of mobility infrastructures through electric vehicles of various types (scooters, cargo bikes, e-cars), which make corresponding supply infrastructures necessary (charging stations, etc.) and a reconceptualization of urban space possible (Doheim, Farag, and Kamel 2020), such as the repurposing of areas previously reserved for parking

(Nieuwenhuijsen and Khreis 2016, 254, 258). But there is a third analytical respect in which we encounter infrastructures in the context of the Anthropocene. This refers to cases where infrastructures are created and planned in direct and positive response to the effects of the Anthropocene. Again, temporality is a crucial factor. However, economic value creation is now no longer based on combating the consequences of climate change, as in the case of changes in mobility and energy infrastructures, but rather on affirming these consequences profitably and exploiting them to create new infrastructures.

Artic Shipping

The example of Artic shipping illustrates what such a "positive" embrace of climate change might look like. Up to now, the Arctic and the Arctic Ocean have been a space that was difficult to penetrate and was not relevant in terms of transportation. To navigate it, that is, to cross it to the East or West, was the subject of much imaginative speculation, but actually realizing this was an almost hopeless undertaking (Müller 2022). Today this is no longer true in the same way. Man has achieved his goal, however, not by the optimization of technologies necessary for it, but because he has behaved in such a way that the materiality of the earth itself has changed.

Due to climate change, the Arctic Ocean is becoming increasingly relevant in terms of geopolitics, military strategy, as well as economic viability. This is due to the decline in sea ice, which is changing the navigability of this region of the world (Østreng et al. 2013; Farré et al. 2014; Aksenov et al. 2017; Lasserre and Faury 2019; Paul 2022).[10] Sea ice, that is, frozen seawater, is very significant for the Earth's climate balance because it reflects sunlight more strongly than dark seawater and therefore protects the oceans from warming; if the amount of sea ice decreases, the oceans become warmer, which leads to a further melting of sea ice. In 1996, the eight Arctic littoral states joined together to form the Arctic Council, namely Canada, Denmark, Finland, Iceland, Norway, Russia, Sweden, and the United States. The Artic Council is a high-level inter-governmental forum that exercises sovereignty over the lands within the Arctic Circle. Significantly, the said eight countries considered themselves "members," while the six Indigenous communities – the Aleut International Association, the Arctic Athabaskan Council, the Gwich'in Council International, the Inuit Circumpolar Council, the Russian Association of Indigenous Peoples of the North, and the Saami Council – were only admitted under the status of "permanent participants."[11] The climate-driven development described above involves very different interests, ranging from access to resources to issues of

10   For further information, see the *Arctic Marine Shipping Assessment 2009 Report*, which was developed under the direction of the Protection of the Artic Marine Environment (PAME) Working Group, one of the six working groups of the Arctic Council (Arctic Council 2009).

11   See also the website of the Artic Council, https:// arctic-council.org/ (accessed August 25, 2022).

great power status (the USA, Russia, and China), tourism destinations (Greenland) to the establishment of previously unused sea routes (Paul 2020, 5). What is at stake here is nothing less than the renegotiation of the routes of world trade and thus a global restructuring of the transport network and the associated relations of proximity and distance.

Already the construction of canals like Suez or Panama, which have organized the connection of Atlantic and Indo-Pacific spaces for more than 100 years (Paul 2020, 5), had drastically relativized the proximity and distance of places. In 1886, Ferdinand de Lesseps, designer of the Suez Canal and initially involved in the construction of the Panama Canal, too, stated that both canals were "two great highways of commerce and civilization" (De Lesseps 1886, 519), which made it possible to transport goods more quickly by connecting the different world regions. While the Suez Canal was said to be the "open door" between Europe or North Africa and South Asia, the Panama Canal opened the connection from Europe and America to China, Japan, and Australia (De Lesseps 1886, 519). Accordingly, de Lesseps already had a tabular listing of the shortened routes due to the Panama Canal. The trip from New York to Vancouver, for example, was reduced to a quarter of the previous distance (→ 6).

Even though the completion of the Panama Canal was delayed for almost twenty years due to planning errors and a financing debacle of the construction company under de Lesseps's leadership (it opened only in 1914), this does not change the visions that accompany such infrastructure projects. History, however, also makes clear "the great lines of tension in world politics that a new high-performance transport route is capable of triggering" (Voigt 1965, 195, my translation). For canals refigure in a fundamental way the geography within a local environment as well as the network of world traffic as a whole (Krajewski 2015, 15).

But what has climate change brought about for the Artic Ocean? The so-called Northeast Passage (the section along the coasts of Siberia is also referred to as the Northern Sea Route) is today already navigable, which is to say, ice-free, for four to five months a year (July to November) on various routes (Paul 2020, 13) (→ 7).

However, the infrastructure necessary for frequent use has not yet been developed, although Russia has high expectations for it (Liu et al. 2021; Paul and Swistek 2022).[12] This is why China — itself not a littoral state of the Artic — supports Russian projects in Siberia in the sense of an "Artic Silk Road"

12   It is also emphasized that the melting sea ice is not seen by Russia solely as an advantage (resource extraction, shipping routes), but also as a "loss of security" (Paul and Swistek 2022, 6), which in turn could promote Kremlin military aggression and thus destabilize the region overall. The new naval doctrine of July 2022 can be seen in this context, which both underlines Russia's claim to be a great maritime power and its ambitions with respect to the Arctic Ocean, is causing concern among the other seven Arctic states, together with China's research activities (Reuters 2022; Spiegel 2022).

6 Distance in miles saved between various ports when using the Panama Canal
(Source: De Lesseps 1886, 519)

7 Arctic Shipping Routes: Northwest Passage (red) and Northeast Passage (yellow)
(Source: Artic Council 2009, 17)

Names of ports.	Distance by Cape Horn.	Distance by Panama canal.	Distance saved.
London or Liverpool to San Francisco	16,900	8,200	8,700
Havre to San Francisco	16,100	7,900	8,200
London to Sydney	16,400	10,900	5,500
Havre to Sydney	16,100	10,600	5,500
Bordeaux or Havre to Valparaiso	10,900	7,450	3,450
London to Sandwich Islands	14,900	7,900	7,000
New York to Valparaiso	10,600	3,900	6,700
New York to Callao	11,200	3,000	8,200
New York to Guayaquil	12,000	2,400	9,600
New York to San Diego	15,400	3,700	11,700
New York to San Francisco	15,900	4,200	11,700
New York to Vancouver	16,600	4,600	12,000

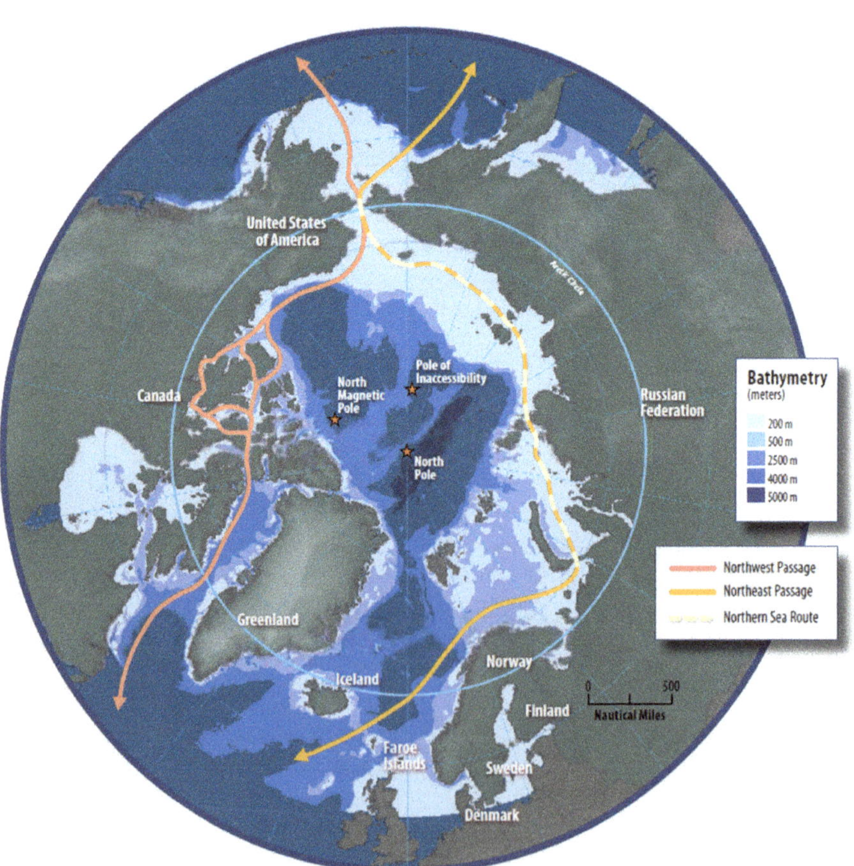

(Lim 2018), but is equally interested in the Northwest Passage, which in turn interferes with Canadian interests that understand it as an internal water route (Lackenbauer et al. 2018). The Northwest Passage is still covered by ice all year round, but it is expected that it will be navigable on up to 130 days a year during the course of the 2030s. At the same time, and in contrast to the Northern Sea Route, there are very branched, different shipping routes through the Canadian archipelago, which comprises 36,000 small and tiny islands whose position respectively could change drastically in geopolitical terms as stations of a navigable Northwest Passage (Paul 2020, 18). The same applies to the Transpolar Sea Route that passes close to the North Pole, which is currently only navigable with heavy icebreakers, but would have the advantage of crossing the high seas and thus international waters, thereby avoiding territorial conflicts. It is expected that this route will be ice-free and thus navigable in the 2040s (Paul 2020, 18). Besides access to resources (coal, oil, gas) or tourist destinations (such as Greenland), it is also about a drastic shortening of transport routes, which would further shrink the world in David Harvey's sense (Harvey 1990, 241). For while a container from Murmansk to Shanghai currently takes 37 days to cover a distance of 12,500 kilometers by sea through the Suez Canal, this would be halved to 18 days and 6,500 kilometers on the Northern Sea Route.[13]

In the case of Arctic shipping, then, climate change is not only leading to a rethinking and a modification of existing infrastructures, as is happening, for example, regarding renewable energy or other forms of urban mobility, but here it is, quite materially, giving rise to entirely new ways of infrastructuring the planet that would not have been possible "without" climate change.

Conclusion

Infrastructures are "in time" in various ways. This concerns their everyday forms of fragility and the activities of care and maintenance directed at them. We have come to know this as the processuality of infrastructures, which can be understood as the work permanently invested in maintaining infrastructures (Schabacher 2022). The background here was the fundamental connection between infrastructures and breakdown, which is not an exception but always affects normal operations and makes infrastructures epistemically understandable in the first place. We have further addressed the aging of infrastructures, seeing how different layers of lifetimes overlap and interfere with each other in complex large-scale technical systems and organizations. Then again, infrastructures that are no longer in use do not simply disappear, but remain in a specific

13   However, connections via the Arctic Sea would not always be more cost-effective than the routes via Suez or Panama, as a shorter route might only be navigable more slowly due to ice conditions (Paul 2020, 19).

way, which has effects on the lifeworlds of those who have to deal with them. This is particularly evident for imperial infrastructures, but also warlike conflicts and ecological catastrophes produce such "ruins." They figure as "material witnesses" (Schuppli), which through their "duress" (Stoler) refer to the historical contexts that produced them. Looking at anthropogenic climate change and how infrastructures are related to it, I have distinguished three types of temporal relations. First, infrastructures are significant contributors to climate change, for instance through the extraction of fossil energy resources, and are thus its primary *causes*. Second, infrastructures *respond* to climate change, for example, by developing alternative energies and forms of mobility. Here, then, they help transform and modify the consequences of climate change, with a focus on reducing its impacts. Finally, with Arctic shipping, we have learned about an example where climate change actually becomes a producer of new infrastructures (transport routes, tourism destinations). Here, in a cynical and short-term manner, there is speculation on how best to *profit from* the changes associated with climate change. To conclude, infrastructures are closely related to anthropogenic climate change: they produce it, they deal with it, and they systematically exploit it. Thus, infrastructures are fundamental mediators of climate change. In their precarious temporality, they are themselves material witnesses to the ecological disasters of this planet.

Aksenov, Yevgeny, Ekaterina E. Popova, Andrew Yool, A.J. George Nurser, et al. 2017. "On the Future Navigability of Arctic Sea Routes: High-resolution Projections of the Arctic Ocean and Sea Ice." *Marine Policy* 75: 300–17.

Aldrich, Mark. 2006. *Death Rode the Rails: American Railroad Accidents and Safety, 1828–1965*. Baltimore, MD: Johns Hopkins University Press.

American Society of Civil Engineers (ACSE). 2021. *2021 Report Card for America's Infrastructure*. Accessed August 24, 2022. https://infrastructurereportcard.org/wp-content/uploads/2020/12/National_IRC_2021-report-2.pdf.

Apel, Dora. 2015. *Beautiful Terrible Ruins: Detroit and the Anxiety of Decline*. New Brunswick, NJ and London: Rutgers University Press.

Artic Council. 2009. *Arctic Marine Shipping Assessment 2009 Report*. Second printing. Accessed August 26, 2022. https://pame.is/images/03_Projects/AMSA/AMSA_2009_report/AMSA_2009_Report_2nd_print.pdf.

BMVI (Bundesministerium für Verkehr und Infrastruktur). 2020. "Pressemitteilung: Bund und DB unterzeichnen größtes Modernisierungsprogramm für das Schienennetz." January 14. Accessed August 24, 2022. https://bmvi.de/SharedDocs/DE/Pressemitteilungen/2020/001-scheuer-starke-schiene-unterzeichnung-lufv.html.

Borrion, Aiduan, Mairi J. Black, and Onemus Mwabonje, eds. 2021. *Life Cycle Assessment: A Metric for the Circular Economy*. Cambridge, UK: Royal Society of Chemistry.

Cairns, Stephen and Jane M. Jacobs. 2014. *Buildings Must Die: A Perverse View of Architecture*. Cambridge, MA/London: MIT Press.

Carruthers, David, ed. 2008. *Environmental Justice in Latin America: Problems, Promise, and Practice*. Cambridge, MA/London: MIT Press.

Chakrabarty, Dipesh. 2009. "The Climate of History: Four Theses." *Critical Inquiry* 35 (2): 197–222.

Clormann, Michael and Nina Klimburg-Witjes. 2022. "Troubled Orbits and Earthly Concerns: Space Debris as a Boundary Infrastructure." *Science, Technology, & Human Values* 47 (5): 960–85.

Cohn, Marisa Leavitt. 2016. "Convivial Decay: Entangled Lifetimes in a Geriatric Infrastructure." In: *Proceedings of the 19th ACM Conference on Computer-Supported Cooperative Work & Social Computing 2016*, 1511–23.

Crutzen, Paul. 2002. "Geology of Mankind." *Nature* 415: 23.

Däumer, Matthias, Aurélia Kalisky, and Heike Schlie, eds. 2017. *Über Zeugen. Szenarien von Zeugenschaft und ihre Akteure*. Paderborn: Fink.

Degeling, Jasmin and Maren Haffke, eds. 2021. *Zeitschrift für Medienwissenschaft 24: Medien der Sorge*.

Deutsche Bahn. 2022. "Pressemitteilung: 13,6 Milliarden Euro für das Neue Netz für Deutschland." Februar 2022. Accessed August 24, 2022. https://deutschebahn.com/de/presse/suche_Medienpakete/13-6-Milliarden-Euro-fuer-das-Neue-Netz-fuer-Deutschland-7250964#.

Doheim, Rahma M., Alshimaa Aboelmakarem Farag, and Ehab Kamel, eds. 2020. *Humanizing Cities Through Car-Free City Development and Transformation*. Hershey, PA: IGI Global.

Engels, Jens Ivo, eds. 2018. *Key Concepts for Critical Infrastructure Research*. Wiesbaden/Heidelberg: Springer VS.

Farré, Albert Buixadé, Scott R. Stephenson, Linling Chen, Michael Czub, et al. 2014. "Commercial Arctic Shipping through the Northeast Passage: Routes, Resources, Governance, Technology, and Infrastructure." *Polar Geography* 37 (4): 298–324.

Forsthoff, Ernst. 1938. *Die Verwaltung als Leistungsträger*. Stuttgart and Berlin: Kohlhammer.

Gladwell, Malcolm. 2000. *The Tipping Point: How Little Things Can Make a Big Difference*. New York, NY: Little Brown.

Graham, Stephen and Nigel Thrift. 2007. "Out of Order: Understanding Repair and Maintenance." *Theory, Culture and Society* 24 (3): 1–25.

Hahn, Hans P. 2018. "Das 'zweite Leben' von Mobiltelefonen und Fahrrädern: Temporalität und Nutzungsweisen technischer Objekte in Westafrika." In: *Kulturen des Reparierens: Dinge—Wissen—Praktiken*, edited by Stefan Krebs, Gabriele Schabacher, and Heike Weber, 105–19. Bielefeld: Transcript.

Haraway, Donna. 2015. "Anthropocene, Capitalocene, Plantationocene, Chthulucene: Making Kin." *Environmental Humanities* 6: 159–65.

Hetherington, Kregg, ed. 2019. *Infrastructure, Environment, and Life in the Anthropocene*. Durham, NC/London: Duke University Press.

Hommels, Anique. 2008. *Unbuilding Cities: Obduracy in Urban Sociotechnical Change*. Cambridge, MA/London: MIT Press.

Horn, Eva. 2018. *The Future as Catastrophe: Imagining Disaster in the Modern Age*. New York, NY/Chichester: Columbia University Press.

Horn, Eva, and Hannes Bergthaller. 2019. *The Anthropocene: Key Issues for the Humanities*. New York, NY/London: Routledge.

Illich, Ivan. 1981. *Shadow Work*. Boston, MA: Boyars.

Kinkartz, Sabine. 2020. "Gesundheitsämter: Mit Papier, Stift und Fax gegen Corona." *DW.com*, January 26. Accessed August 24, 2022. https://dw.com/de/gesundheits%C3%A4mter-mit-papier-stift-und-fax-gegen-corona/a-56347106.

Koch, Lars, Tobias Nanz, and Johannes Pause. 2018. "Imagined Scenarios of Disruption: A Concept." In: *Disruption in the Arts. Textual, Visual, and Performative Strategies for Analyzing Societal Self-Descriptions*, edited by Lars Koch, Tobias Nanz, and Johannes Pause, 68–81. Berlin/Boston, MA: De Gruyter.

Krajewski, Markus. 2015. *World Projects: Global Information before World War I*. Minneapolis, MN: University of Minnesota Press.

Krämer, Sybille. 2015. *Media, Messenger, Transmission. An Approach to Media Philosophy*. Amsterdam: Amsterdam University Press.

Larkin, Brian. 2008. "Degraded Images, Distorted Sounds: Nigerian Video and the Infrastructure of Piracy." In: *Signal and Noise. Media, Infrastructure, and Urban Culture in Nigeria*, by Brian Larkin, 217–41. Durham, NC/London: Duke University Press.

Lasserre, Frédéric and Olivier Faury, eds. 2019. *Arctic Shipping: Climate Change, Commercial Traffic and Port Development*. London: Routledge.

Latour, Bruno. 1993. *We Have Never Been Modern*. Cambridge, MA: Harvard University Press.

Latour, Bruno. 1996. "Trains of Thought: Piaget, Formalism, and the Fifth Dimension." *Common Knowledge* 6 (3): 170–91.

Latschan, Thomas. 2022. "Ukraine: Will the Railroad be what decides the war?" *DW Europe*, May 6. Accessed August 24, 2022. https://dw.com/p/4AwqV.

Lesseps, Ferdinand. 1886. "The Panama Canal." *Science* 8 (200): 517–20.

Levine, Philip and Andrew Moore. 2010. *Detroit Disassembled*. Photography by Andrew Moore. Essay by Philip Levine. Bologna: Damiani.

Lim, Kong Soon. 2018. "China's Arctic Policy and the Polar Silk Road Vision." In: *Arctic Yearbook 2018*, edited by L. Heininen and H. Exner-Pirot, 420–32. Akureyri, Iceland: Northern Research Forum.

Lyons, Siobhan, ed. 2018. *Ruin Porn and the Obsession with Decay*. Cham: Palgrave Macmillan.

Malefakis, Alexis. 2018. "'Tansanier mögen keine unversehrten Sachen': Reparaturen und ihre Spuren an alten Schuhen in Daressalam, Tansania." In: *Kulturen des Reparierens: Dinge—Wissen—Praktiken*, edited by Stefan Krebs, Gabriele Schabacher, and Heike Weber, 303–26. Bielefeld: Transcript.

McDonough, William and Michael Braungart. 2002. *Cradle to Cradle. Remaking the Way We Make Things*. New York, NY: North Point Press.

Moore, Jason W. 2017. "Confronting the Popular Anthropocene: Toward an Ecology of Hope." *New Geographies* 9: 186–91.

Moore, Jason W. ed. 2016. *Anthropocene or Capitalocene? Nature, History, and the Crisis of Capitalism*. Oakland, CA: PM Press.

Müller, Dorit. 2022. *Polarreisen. Zwischen Empire und Imagination*. Berlin: Kadmos.

Neubert, Christoph. 2012. "Störung." In: *Handbuch der Mediologie: Signaturen des Medialen*, edited by Christina Bartz, Ludwig Jäger, Marcus Krause, and Erika Linz, 272–88. Munich: Fink.

Nieuwenhuijsen, Mark and Haneen Khreis. 2016. "Car Free Cities: Pathway to Healthy Urban Living." *Environment International* 94: 251–62.

Nixon, Rob. 2011. *Slow Violence and the Enironmentalism of the Poor*. Cambridge, MA: Harvard University Press.

Østreng, Willy, Karl Magnus Eger, Brit Fløistad, Arnfinn Jørgensen-Dahl, et al. 2013. *Shipping in Arctic Waters: A Comparison of the Northeast, Northwest and Trans Polar Passages*. Heidelberg: Springer.

Otto, Friederike. 2020. *Angry Weather: Heat Waves, Floods, Storms, and the New Science of Climate Change*. Vancouver: Greystone Books.

Parikka, Jussi. 2014. *The Anthrobscene*. Minneapolis, MN: University of Minnesota Press.

Parks, Lisa. 2013. "Orbital Ruins." *NECSUS. European Journal of Media Studies* 2 (2): 419–29.

Paul, Michael. 2020. *Arktische Seewege: zwiespältige Aussichten im Nordpolarmeer*. Berlin: Stiftung Wissenschaft und Politik.

Paul, Michael. 2022. *Der Kampf um den Nordpol: Die Arktis, der Klimawandel und die Rivalität der Großmächte*, Freiburg, Basel and Vienna: Herder.

Paul, Michael and Göran Swistek. 2022. *Russia in the Artic. Development Plans, Military Potential, and Conflict Prevention*. Berlin: Stiftung Wissenschaft und Politik. German Institute for International and Security Affairs.

Perrow, Charles. 1984. *Normal Accidents: Living With High-Risk Technologies*. New York, NY: Basic Books.

Potthast, Jörg. 2008. "Ethnography of a Paper Strip: The Production of Air Safety, Science." *Technology & Innovation Studies* 4 (1): 47–68.

Puig de la Bellacasa, María. 2017. *Matters of Care: Speculative Ethics in More Than Human Worlds*. Minneapolis, MN/London: University of Minnesota Press.

Reichle, Ingrid, ed. 2021. *Plastic Ocean: Art and Science Responses to Marine Pollution*. Berlin: De Gruyter.

Reuters. 2022. "On Navy Day, Putin says United States is main threat to Russia." July 31, Reuters.com. Accessed August 28, 2022, https://reuters.com/business/aerospace-defense/putin-says-russian-navy-get-new-hypersonic-missiles-soon-2022-07-31/.

Rinaldi, Steven M., James P. Peerenboom, and Terrence K. Kelly. 2001. "Identifying, Understanding, and Analyzing Critical Infrastructure Interdependencies." *IEEE Control Systems Magazine* (Dec.): 11–25.

Rothöhler, Simon. 2021. *Medien der Forensik*. Bielefeld: Transcript.

Schabacher, Gabriele. 2022. *Infrastruktur-Arbeit: Kulturtechniken und Zeitlichkeit der Erhaltung*, Berlin: Kadmos.

Schabacher, Gabriele. 2021. "Time and Technology: The Temporalities of Care." In: *Media Infrastructures and the Politics of Digital Time: Essays on Hardwired Temporalities*, edited by Axel Volmar and Kyle Stine, 55–75. Amsterdam: Amsterdam University Press.

Schabacher, Gabriele. 2020. "Waiting: Cultural Techniques, Media and Infrastructures." In: *Cultural Techniques: Spaces, Texts, Collectives*, edited by Jörg Dünne, Kathrin Fehringer, Kristina Kuhn, and Wolfgang Struck, 71–84. London/New York, NY: De Gruyter.

Schabacher, Gabriele. 2019. "Staged Wrecks: The Railroad Crash between Infrastructural Lesson and Amusement." In: *Infrastructuring Publics*, edited by Matthias Korn, Wolfgang Reißmann, Tobias Röhl, and David Sittler, 185–206. Wiesbaden: Springer VS.

Schabacher, Gabriele. 2018. "Abandoned Infrastructures: Technical Networks beyond Nature and Culture." *Zeitschrift für Medien- und Kulturforschung* 9 (1): 127–45.

Schuppli, Susan. 2020. *Material Witness: Media, Forensics, Evidence*. Cambridge/MA: MIT Press.

Schüttpelz, Erhard. 2002. "Eine Umschrift der Störung: Shannons Flußdiagramm der Kommunikation in ihrem kybernetischen Verlauf." In: *Transkribieren: Medien / Lektüre*, edited by Ludwig Jäger and Georg Stanitzek, 233–80. Munich: Fink.

Spiegel. 2022. "Putin schürt mit neuer Marinedoktrin Ängste: USA als 'größte Gefahr'." July 31. Spiegel online. Accessed August 28, 2022. https://spiegel.de/ausland/putin-erlaesst-neue-marine-doktrin-usa-als-groesste-gefahr-a-9db6dab0-9115-4a95-b674-d7b552bcbf99.

Star, Susan Leigh and Karen Ruhleder. 1996. "Steps Toward an Ecology of Infrastructure: Design and Access to Large Information Spaces." *Information Systems Research* 7 (1): 111–34.

Star, Susan Leigh, and Anselm Strauss. 1999. "Layers of Silence, Arenas of Voice: The Ecology of Visible and Invisible Work." *Computer Supported Cooperative Work* 8: 9–30.

Stark, John. 2015. *Product Lifecycle Management 1: 21st Century Paradigm for Product Realisation*. 3rd ed., London: Springer.

Steffen, Will, Jacques Grinevald, Paul Crutzen, and John McNeill. 2011. "The Anthropocene: Conceptual and Historical Perspectives." *Philosophical Transactions of the Royal Society* 369: 842–67.

Stöger, Georg. 2015. "Premodern Sustainability? The Secondhand and Repair Trade in Urban Europe." In: *Cycling and Recyling: Histories of Sustainable Practices*, edited by Ruth Oldenziel and Helmuth Trischler, 147–67. New York, NY/Oxford: Berghahn.

Stoler, Ann Laura. 2016. *Duress: Imperial Durabilities in Our Times*. Durham, NC/London: Duke University Press.

Thompson, Michael. 1979. *Rubbish Theory: The Creation and Destruction of Value*. Oxford: Oxford University Press.

Vehlken, Sebastian. 2020. "The Great Pacific Garbage Catch: Müll als Medium einer 'Plastic Oceanography'." *Zeitschrift für Medienwissenschaft* 23: 84–98.

Virilio, Paul. 1994. *Bunker Archeology*, originally published 1975. New York, NY: Princeton Architectural Press.

Virilio, Paul. 2002. *Ce qui arrive. Publié à l'occasion de l'exposition* Ce qui arrive, *conçue par Paul Virilio, présentée à la Fondation Cartier pour l'art contemporain, à Paris, du 29 novembre 2002 au 30 mars 2003*. Arles: Actes Sud.

Virilio, Paul. 2007. *The Original Accident*. Malden, MA/Cambridge, UK: Polity Press.

Voigt, Fritz. 1963. *Verkehr. Zweiter Band. Erste Hälfte: Die Entwicklung des Verkehrssystems*. Berlin: Duncker & Humblot.

Weizman, Eyal. 2017. *Forensic Architecture: Violence at the Threshold of Detectability*. New York, NY: Zone Books.

Whitehouse, Tanya. 2018. *How Ruins Acquire Aesthetic Value: Modern Ruins, Ruin Porn, and the Ruin Tradition*. Cham: Palgrave Macmillan.

Wynne, Brian. 1988. "Unruly Technology: Practical Rules, Impractical Discourses and Public Understanding." *Social Studies of Science* 18: 147–67.

Yusoff, Kathryn. 2018. *A Billion Black Anthropocenes or None*. Minneapolis, MN: University of Minnesota Press.

Zalasiewicz, Jan, Colin N. Waters and Mark Williams. 2014. "Human Bioturbation, and the Subterranean Landscape of the Anthropocene." *Anthropocene* 6: 3–9.

There is a Crossing, Which is Not a Crossing

at All:
Notes on *AAA Cargo*

Solveig Qu Suess and Jakob Claus

The essay revolves around Solveig Suess's film *AAA Cargo*. It is intended as a collection of fragmented thoughts, quotes, and stills from the film, impressions of watching narrative images, and more theoretical lines of flight. We have arranged a network of reflections on filmmaking, Chinese pop culture, the tensions of infrastructure, and what it means to follow informal logisticians. The essay draws on Solveig's artistic research practice and visual ethnography and thereby navigates media infrastructures, their environments, and the political questions which arise from the often hollow promises of logistics. Infrastructural visions are thus confronted with environmental dynamics and the specificity of unruly material.

Keywords: Logistics, Transportation, Artistic Practice, Media Ecology, Ethnography

85

Entry Points

There is a void between the projected visions and the political goals of the Belt and Road Initiative and lived experience in proximity to large scale infrastructure and economic dynamics. It is within this void where *AAA Cargo* finds its entry points and narrative threads. Fred Moten and Stefano Harney described logistics' aims to erase human elements and provocatively asked where this ambition derives from (Harney and Moten 2013, 92). But one could also ask what forms of on-site work, lively experiences, more-than-human connections, flow into and perhaps even flourish within these burgeoning logistical networks? [I]

[I] Trace personas and ghost murmurings from risk assessments, weather monitoring, credit ratings, your next possible purchase, his favorite color, feedback into concrete, metal, security, boundary forming protocols, building a synchronization of histories which sediment into the discursive infrastructures we find ourselves in. An endless doubling effect, it hides the idea that the construction of right here is built of elsewheres.

The most paralyzing aspect when grasping the hegemonic imagination of the Belt and Road Initiative as an infrastructural mega project is its totalization. [II] Thus, one needs to find submerged ways of access and entry points. Tracing the tension between scales and perspectives can be productive as it opens entry points and gives the possibility of dismantling totalizing views. One of the first encounters of the Belt and Road Initiative during the research was over WeChat, with a logistician called "AAA Cargo". [III] They provided very speedy and cheap services, including distributing sensitive materials that are normally difficult to move on the geographies of the new silk roads. Their service and quasi-legal practice explain how logistics can be hacked by utilizing the access and resources of UPS or DHL for example.

[II] The five continental, mega-infrastructure project is collectively known as the Belt and Road Initiative (BRI), which includes the development of telecommunication cables, railways, dams, and power stations. BRI's massive campaign also provides funds and a labor force to implement these projects predominantly across the Global South, securing more than US$340 billion worth of construction contracts in over 60 countries.

[III] I met "AAA Cargo" through a chat group on the social media platform, WeChat, shortly before embarking on this road-trip to film. A friend had introduced me to a few e-commerce groups which hosted virtual marketplaces offering products and services at wholesale prices. In these groups, active members like Jose, sold VPN routers, or Mc Spade, marketing a substantial inventory of Apple products, another business with expedited

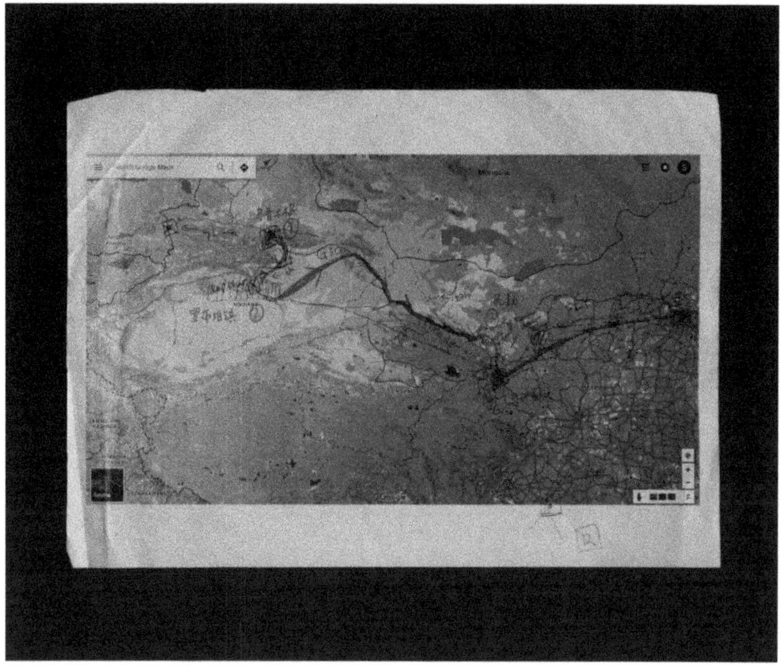

VISAs on offer. These are groups which seemed to be mobilizing circuits of the unfaithful. The "echo chambers" of WeChat chat-rooms. Though it was the repeated announcement of a door-to-door distribution service, by means of different forms of transport, able to send ordinary, copied, battery, liquids, food, sensitive materials from China and beyond – which had arrested my attention.[1]

1   Excerpts taken from Solveig Qu Suess 2018.

Andrei Daler – an informal logistician – explains how the Belt and Road Initiative brings across new policies. Elimination of counterfeit goods and more rational distribution of goods, commodities, and cargo is one of the "soft" directives that comes in the wake of infrastructures. For informal logisticians, it depends on *who* they know to make a small business out of the surplus space in containers. They find means to access these new infrastructures of the Belt and Road, despite the project not designing them as their main users. They know the porosities of logistics. Micro-movements, micro-tactics, micro-experiences.[IV]

[IV] If we pause for a second, and listen in line of sight to the warehouse over there, we might just be able to hear the movements of a work-force, remaining largely hidden behind these container boxes and storage shelves. Long-distance connections nurtured, this time through a mode and means of navigation made otherwise. It seemed that this same apparatus, when looked at with more detail, also creates new opportunities for quasi-legal cargo mobilities, leveraged in the ambiguous pool of gray. Paralogisticians, consisting of Alibaba merchants forming the new generation of precarious workers, developmental refugees forced out of their hometowns, bandits who refuse to pay taxes. They hack infrastructural spaces through trans-generational *guanxi*[2] and long-distance friendships. Renegotiating within airports, markets, warehouses, special economic zones. Here, the imagining of the unimaginable, is an everyday method of making ends meet.

Assembled Voices

I've been thinking about the narrative voice as it introduces an observing, diary-like, informing, but sometimes even funny or absurd tone. I listen, read and watch the film at the same time, which carries an effect of overwhelming superimposition.[V, VI] While the scenes with the animated bubbles distill a tranquilizing effect.

[V] There are two main scripted threads that arise out of the interviews and segments that I've inserted in between. One of the threads is based on my field notes which do not necessarily have a very linear or coherent narrative, but for me communicate a feeling of the space and landscapes that I went through.

"It's 3p.m., and we're on the road again.

People sometimes mention that whole towns vanish for the saving of three hours travel time.

'The sand moves an average of ten meters per year from each side, sometimes reaching twenty meters'

Sand renders time into recursions. It does not stop; it only rests.

When looking out at them, I think about how easy it is for these landscapes to collude with wind."[3]

The new railway undulates accordingly. Criss-crossed screens pattern alongside its tracks. Sand-control infrastructures that stall the flow of the land aim not to obliterate the desert as such, but, for the moment, to stall it in a holding pattern actively poised against sand's futures. The sands remind us of deserts growing from modern peripheries.

[VI] To evoke something that feminist scholar Donna J. Haraway (2016) puts into words, storytelling is a process of thinking. It does not conclude but instead the process is part of the practice. And this resonated a lot with how we think about filmmaking, which is very process-based, not just in how the story is crafted but also in the time and spaces that are connected through moving images, or the people that we organize and share the research, experience, and work with.

2   In Chinese, *guanxi* refers to the nature of personal and business networks. Unlike in the West, *guanxi* relationships are almost never established purely through formal meetings but must also include spending time to get to know people during tea sessions, dinner banquets, karaoke nights, etc. *Guanxi* requires a personal bond before any business relationship can develop. "A person who has a great deal of *guanxi* will be better positioned to generate business than someone who lacks it" (See: https://investopedia.com/terms/g/guanxi.asp, accessed June 30, 2022).

3   Unless otherwise noted all quotes are excerpts taken from *AAA Cargo*, Solveig Qu Suess, 2018, 34 mins.

The voices are assembled from a multiplicity of selves. For example, there are logisticians talking about the network of informal traders who find ways to become users of the infrastructural project even though it wasn't designed for them. This script is informed by those fragments and collages together a collective intelligence.[VII]

"'Overland, there's shorter time to dream,' she sighs, staring into the blue-green abyss of her iPhone screen.

Echoing back is the muted tapping of agile fingers.

Dear friend, amazing products await you!
Dear friend, today everybody gets a gift!
Teeth Whitening, Hair Removal, Hair Growth, New Original
Gadgets, Quality Goods and more…
Good mood guaranteed!

We hasten through an invisible geography whose features constantly shift beneath our feet.

Place names are irrelevant, monuments indistinct.

The New Silk Road paves the way elsewhere, leaving a trail of suspended conversations, synthetic debris, and scattered sand."

[VII] "The production of one irreality upon the other and the play of non-sense (which is not mere meaninglessness) upon meaning may therefore help to relieve the basic referent of its occupation, for the present situation of critical inquiry seems much less one of attacking the illusion of reality as one of displacing and emptying out the establishment of totality." (Trinh T. Minh-ha 1991, 50)

Bubbles of Future Capital
As part of the Belt and Road Initiative, one of the railroad tracks which begin from Chongqing, China and ends at Duisburg, Germany was constructed in collaboration between the Chinese state and Hewlett Packard. It follows a very particular logic within China in regard to the initiative to "develop" the whole province of Xinjiang, the home of the Turkic Muslim Uyghurs. Hewlett Packard took the chance to use the direct connection to the European market out of the special economic zone in Xinjiang. In contrast to the promised development, workers were sleeping on their desks, their screensavers displaying calm and continuous bubbles. But still, everyone was holding onto the promises and dreams of infrastructure bringing productivity. There is an almost endless pending or waiting for wealth to come. The markets will boom soon.

Stills from *AAA Cargo*, Solveig Qu Suess, 2018, 34 mins., courtesy of the artist

skilled navigators

veins and sinews

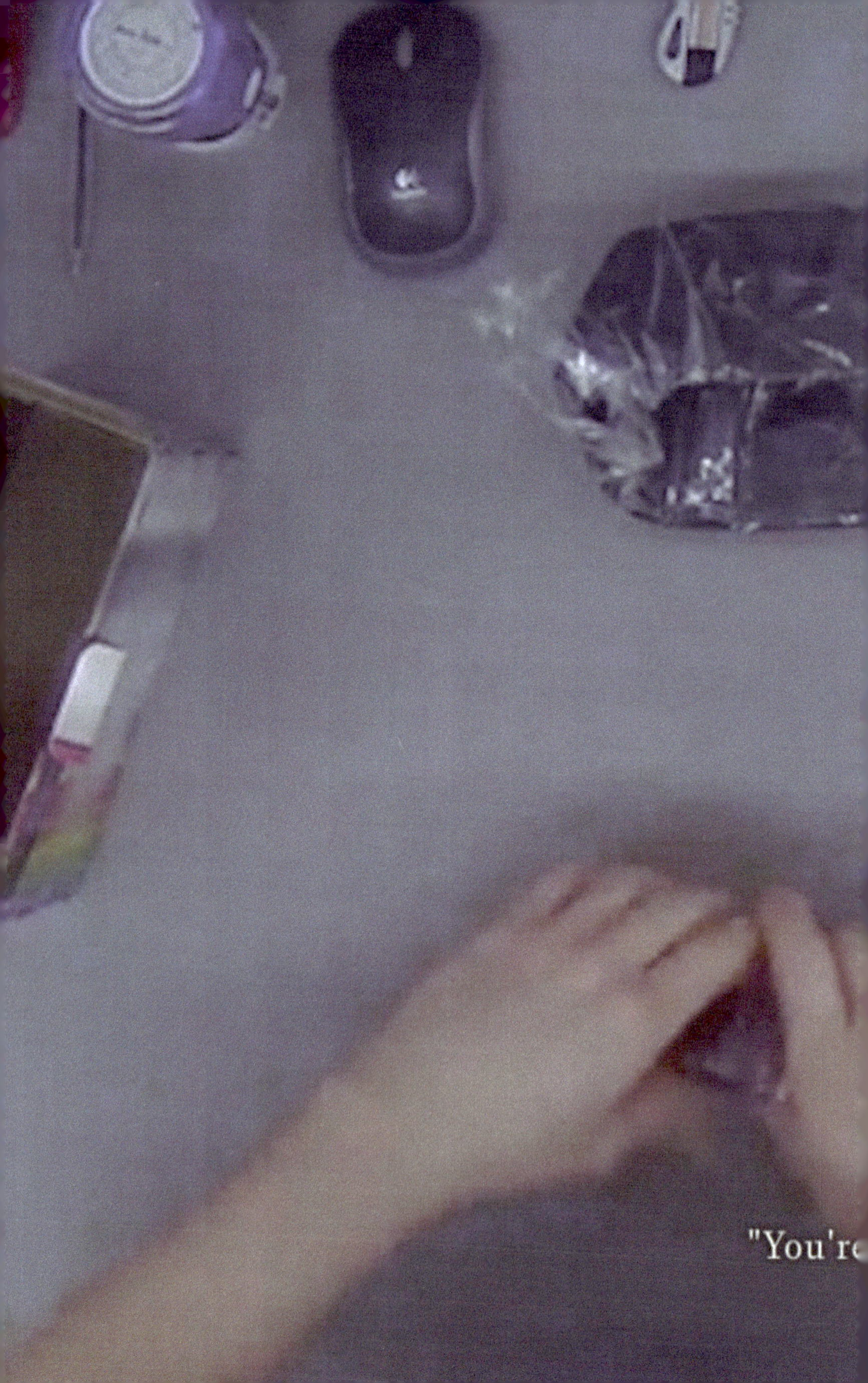
"You're

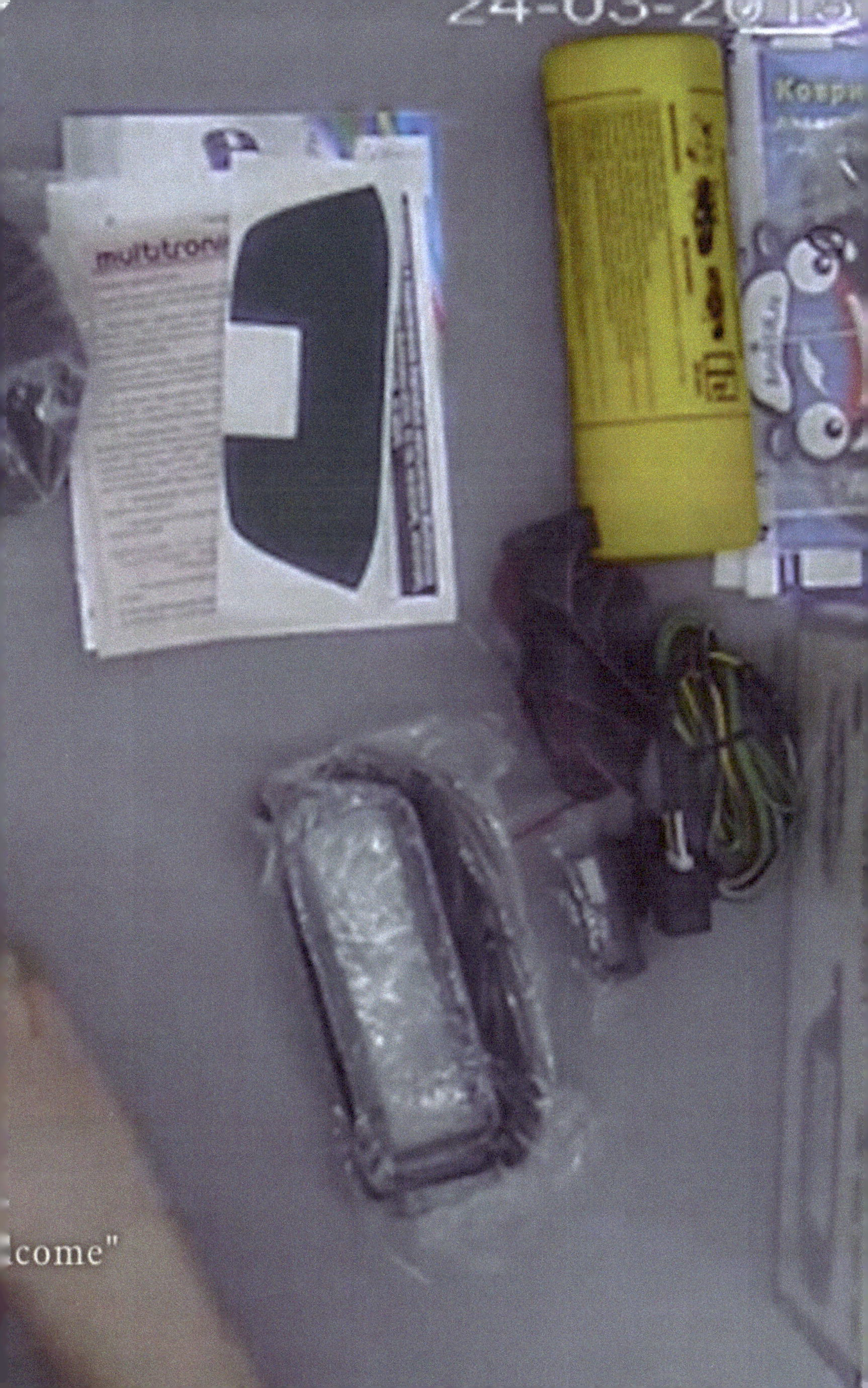
24-03-2015
multitronic
"come"

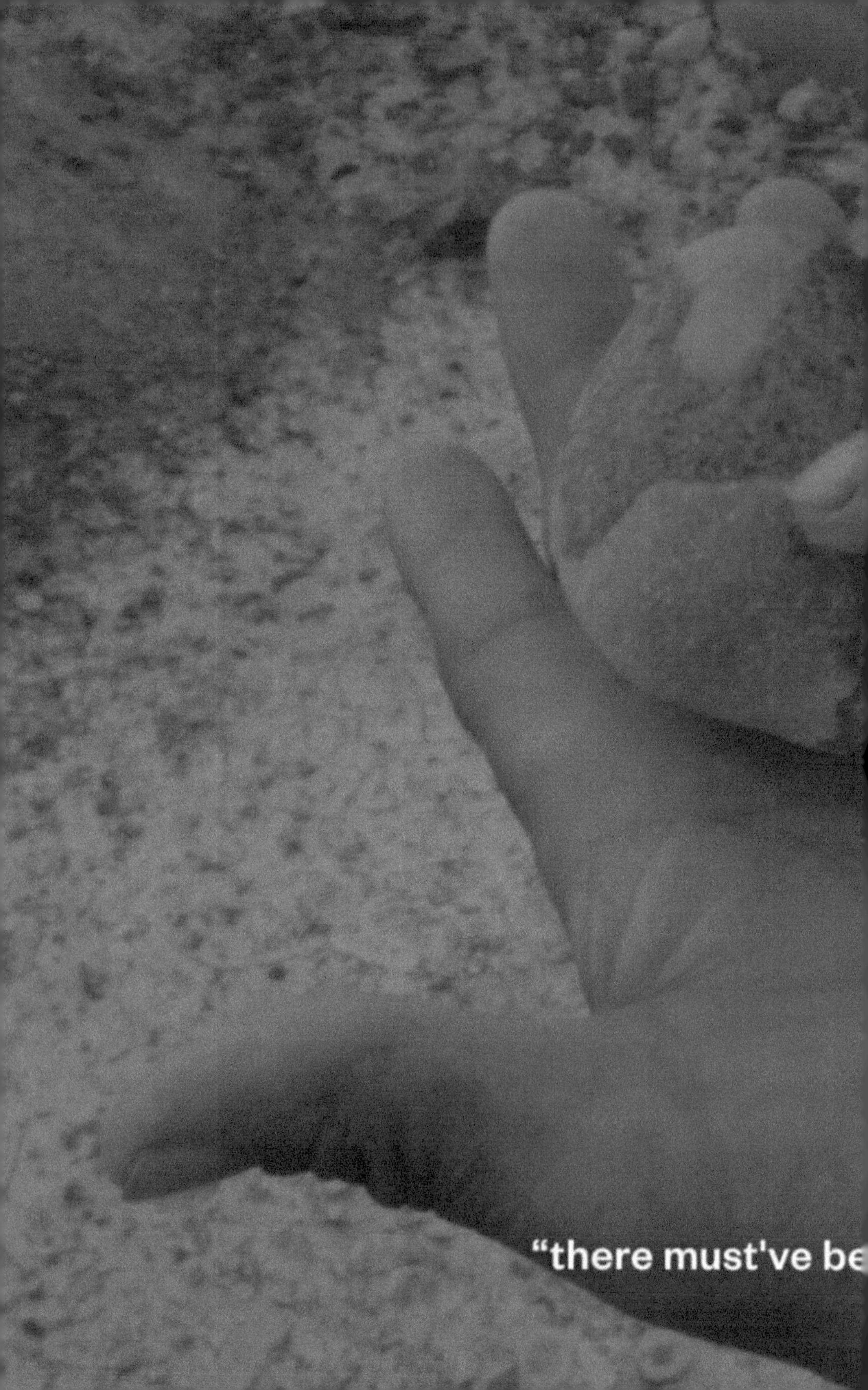
"there must've be

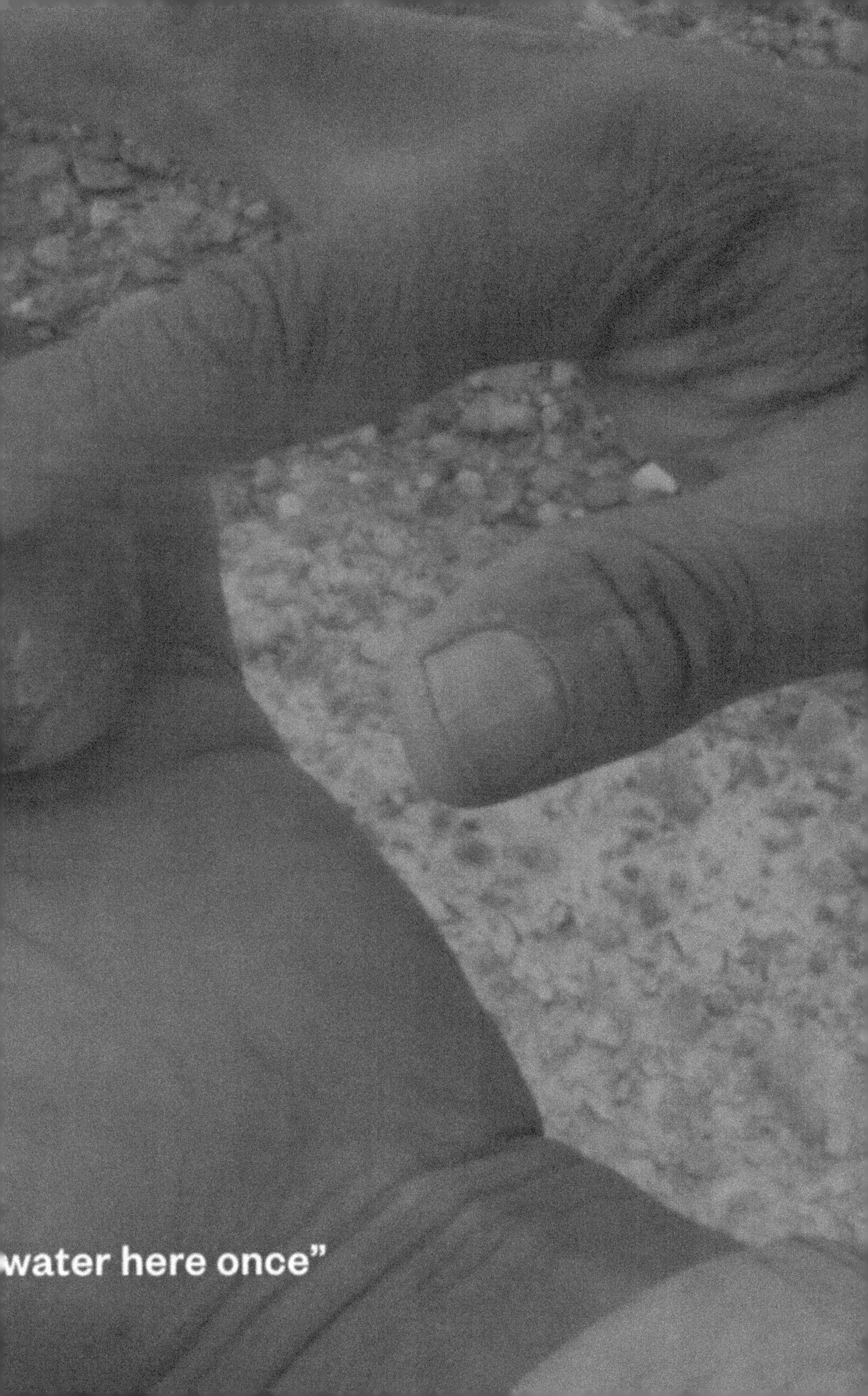
water here once"

The promise of productivity and capital to come is a trope *AAA Cargo* negotiates via sound. Elevator music bridges consumerism and labor, as both can be framed and governed as acts of patience and waiting with the idea of pacification and potential prosperity. Since elevator music is especially popular in China in the retail sector, it re-entered the film in the form of sloweddown Kenny G.[XIII]

[XIII] There is a moment in *AAA Cargo* where the song *Going Home*, by the American smooth jazz saxophonist Kenny G, plays over animated bubbles as they float over a concrete road. The song was a very reworked version of it – looped, sped up, slowed down. But his music might conjure a lot of nostalgia from anyone who grew up in East or Southeast Asia during the '90s, when his albums were kept on loop in newly opened shopping centers, with his song *Going Home* used to announce the opening and closing of shops. There's a certain sense of pacification which arises through muzak – smooth elevator jazz – conjured when waiting for the arrival of capital and markets, placating the public. The bubbles placed along with the Kenny G song together obliquely refer to David Harvey's (2005) theory of the "spatio-temporal fix."[4]

4   **David Harvey introduces the term to name the capitalist logic that surplus productivity needs a purpose or fix in the form of new/ future (temporal) geographies (space) that can absorb this surplus.**

The construction of infrastructures doesn't necessarily follow any practical reason but can pacify social and labor unrest, unemployment and asymmetrical resources.[IX] Infrastructure could be read in analogy to the impro-jazzy-muzak.

[IX] He spoke about how by the pure act of constructing high-speed rail lines, highways, dams and water projects, new airports and container terminals, would be used to pacify social instability and sustain their overall GDP. The "spatio-temporal fix" would provide employment for surpluses of capital and labor while using up the extra tons of steel and concrete, and reinforcing the spatial designs of capital accumulation. A subduing of any forms of unruly behavior, through the promise and fantasy brought forth by infrastructure.

Emptiness

New roads are being constructed alongside the railroad tracks, but because of the tolls and restrictions of movement one witnesses an asymmetrical power dynamic between who can and who can't access railroad tracks and roads. The same dynamic affects small towns in between bigger hubs and cities, which are unable to sustain their livelihoods because of the changing routes. Power geometries are becoming visible here.[X]

[X] "How do mechanisms of control impact mobility, and the mobility of whom? Something as simple as a road or a railroad track is not only a thing or object, but also a relation. They are the physical networks through which goods, ideas, waste, power, people, and finance are trafficked, while also being complex processes that constantly open up possibilities as

2   Windows 10 Bubbles Screensaver (Source: Winaero, 2016 https://winaero.com/customize-screen-savers-in-windows-10-using-secret-hidden-options, accessed June 30, 2022)

3   DB Schenker: Ocean Freight (Source: https://youtube.com/watch?v=I5sWn2ASHNw, accessed June 30, 2022)

both inclusion and exclusion. Closeness is not necessarily about distance between here and there, but rather how close things are is defined by parameters, disagreements, arguments, revenues, personal histories, associations, and importantly, race." (Suess 2021, 33)

There is a crossing, which is not a crossing at all. It consists of two or more disconnected channels in the form of streets running under high-speed railroad tracks. From below one can see the pillars – concrete with different forms and functions. Various directions in distinctly separated spaces, with no possibility to meet. A perfect intersection – if you look at it on a map.

Do people disappear?

The distinctive feeling of emptiness across logistical sites act as another important entry point into the hegemonic structure. But actually, the roads and railroad tracks are anything but empty, as these structures are inhabited by subtle movements that humans can't easily register. People do not completely disappear; infrastructure and logistics were simply very good at hiding "the elsewhere" and "its other." Especially in Xinjiang the labor camps as well as workers literally disappear in many people's eyes, but they're always there. A kind of ghostly presence.[XI]

[XI] "Under the banner of 'emptiness,' and the inanity that 'there is nothing at all in the desert,' those living in occupied deserts have been forcibly displaced, de-nomadized, and in some cases exterminated – either immediately or gradually. As environmental critic Rob Nixon argues in his book *Slow Violence and the Environmentalism of the Poor*, maintaining media attention on the temporalities of toxicity is challenging: 'not only because it is spectacle deficient, but also because the fallout's impact may range from the cellular to the transnational and (depending on the specific character of the chemical or radiological hazard) may stretch beyond the horizon of imaginable time." (Henni 2022, 13)

Next to/Surrounding the Frame
When is it the right moment to begin recording a scene? How should the relationship between sound and image be understood in relation to the spaces being framed? What is enabled when these elements are separated?[XII]

Humans are often absent from the image, speaking from beyond the frame. Some of the people that I interviewed entered the frame after or before our conversation took place. People moving goods and cargo, blurry gestures in conversation with materiality. To focus on recording bodily movement rather than capturing their bodies, was a way to negotiate the extractive inheritance of observing people with a camera. It then becomes less about detecting bodies but more about registering their movements within certain spaces. Like a triangulation of image, sound, and time.[XIII]

[XII] "The aesthetics of the frame is equally invested in the dynamic interaction between realities captured on camera and the procedures of framing. Ultimately, however, the performative interaction suggested here departs from the representational paradigm." (Hongisto 2015, 15)

[XIII] "Montage as a technique can work to reassert the fragmentary when engaging with the hegemonic calculations made through imaging technologies. With the possibility to link and make explicit connections between geographies, things and events that are typically left obfuscated within the new conditions of modernity." (Suess 2021, 34)

Interscalar Devices

"It's 10 a.m. in Beijing.
The sky turned grey and the smell of dust and sand crept into my room this morning."

We see a lot of hands; people moving around and doing things with their hands. These frames are intersected with scenes from desert landscapes and their different temporal layers.[XIV] One learns that the desert is not behaving like it's supposed to in order for the infrastructural buildings to function smoothly. The narrator says: sand is always moving in recursion and never stops, but only rests. Against the rhythmic traffic on railroads and highways the sand follows its own pattern of movement and inscribes itself within concrete structures and their surroundings.

[XIV] How can we undo our modern geographies of concealment and bring into view the lattice of relations, often very violent ones, that sustain modern states and international markets?[5]

5   See XqSu 2021.

The new railroad and highway routes cut through the Gobi and Taklamakan deserts. Historically, these spaces have also been where mass irrigation experiments have taken place, mobilized with the rhetoric of deserts being empty and their need to be developed. Many socialist projects were aimed at the creation of infrastructure and plantations in that area.[XV] One of the manifold consequences has been that lakes dried out and the occurrence of sandstorms increased rapidly. Sand storms that used to occur once every 14 years started occurring every year. Flights get canceled, railroads blocked and the desire for frictionless movement is confronted with impediments. The sand storms are an interesting character in the story because their movements enact what is like a post-colonial revenge, in the sense that they reappear from a suppressed past and carry with them ongoing contaminants gathered from the industrial zones they travel across.[XVI]

[XV] "From the late 1950s, the Northwest China and Inner Mongolia Autonomous Region Desertification Control Plan outlined a 'desertification' governance system whose policies and regulations called on local government departments, communities, and social groups to participate in controlling the desert. Control in this context meant modulating the advancement of the desert, stalling how sand encroached across the region. Sand 'does not stop; it only rests.' Control was thus the ability to manage the relation between time and distance." (XqSu 2022, 230)

[XVI] "Distinctive patterns of colonialism were encoded within the modernist project of Chinese Communism. Projects, such as the Three-North Shelter Forest Program, produced and were produced by the concept of the frontier, where the young settlers' transformation of peripheral landscapes into productive spaces were important in securing the state's influence in China's peripheries. The frontier was crucial in defining the perimeters of national borders, with its power lying in the prospect of extraction and in the material manipulation of its environmental conditions." (XqSu 2022, 230)

Sand storms don't abide by social borders or laws.

How does the environment interact with man-made structures, how does the landscape inscribe itself into planned grids, tarplanes, and door sealings?[XVII]

[XVII] Calculations of speed and smoothness along corporate supply chains have woven together the state's biopolitical control of the local Uyghur, Indigenous, and ethnic minority populations with its fight against increasingly strange weather. Though by the design and engineering of immediate time and space, the long-term, delayed effects of industry and capital form what Rob Nixon would call a "temporal disjuncture," a dislocation of causal relations across space. Such geographies of concealment diffuse and obscure the truly global nature of settler colonial dispossession and genocide. Seemingly separate ecological, labor, and Indigenous struggles can be unified in the collective struggle against settler coloniality.

Considering the dust storm as a method gestures toward what historian Gabrielle Hecht describes as a multi-scalar approach – to "move between scales while simultaneously attending to the history and politics of scalemaking" (Hecht 2018, 114). In this case, the dust storm as an inter-scalar vehicle undoes the idea that the above scales can be seen as distinct

4   5   Still from *Spring in the Desert (Shamo De Chuntian* 沙漠的春天*)*, Zhu Wenshun, 1975,
(Source: https://youtube.com/watch?v=t3e2-F6Tqf8, accessed June 30, 2022)

at all, not only on a narrative level, but materially as well. Scale-as-method thus pulls into relation time and spaces which have long been kept separate.[XVIII]

[XVIII] "By thinking with duration, montage and defamiliarization, these techniques can become conceptual tools to account for the relational and material aspects of infrastructure and the realities it mobilizes. These can be powerful when trying to articulate the different scales of connections with something so abstract like global capital, where the distances between sites and their relations are very blurred, convoluted and planetary.

Filmmaking in many ways, can be an embodied method of researching, mapping, and maybe more accurately – 'unmapping' the complex relations of global capitalism. I see it both as a practice of unstitching and re-stitching: with some films focused on trying to grapple the need to undo our modern geographies of concealment, where things such as environmental issues are kept separate from supply chain expansions and extractive activities, and the importance of bringing into view the matrices of relations that sustain modern states and international markets. While other films aim to create spaces for 'seeing' the familiar, differently, allowing questions to arise on their own terms." (Suess 2021, 35)

Solveig Qu Suess: I would like acknowledge and thank my many collaborators, editors, friends, and family who have contributed to these iterative thoughts on understanding choreographies of space and time through film. Most notably, the publishing team of Lausan, Samia Henni with Isabelle C. Kirkham-Lewitt and Joanna Joseph, Ming Lin and Jerry Zee.

Haraway, Donna J. 2016. *Staying with the Trouble: Making Kin in the Chthulucene*. Durham, NC/London: Duke University Press.

Harney, Stefano, and Fred Moten. 2013. *The Undercommons: Fugitive Planning & Black Study*. Wivenhoe: Minor Compositions.

Harvey, David. 2005. *The New Imperialism*. Oxford: Oxford University Press.

Hecht, Gabrielle. 2018. "Interscalar Vehicles for an African Anthropocene: On Waste, Temporality, and Violence." *Cultural Anthropology* 33 (1): 109–41.

Henni, Samia. 2022. "Against the Regime of 'Emptiness.'" In *Deserts Are Not Empty*, edited by Samia Henni, 11–20. New York, NY: Columbia University Press.

Hongisto, Ilona. 2015. *Soul of the Documentary*. Amsterdam: Amsterdam University Press.

Suess, Solveig Qu. 2018. "AAA Cargo: Notes from the Undercurrent." Presented at the Sonic Acts, Amsterdam. Accessed June 30, 2022. https://youtube.com/watch?v=Mp06Y-vhm6m8.

Suess, Solveig Qu. 2021. "Towards a Documentary-Led Research." In *Signals & Storms - A 6-Week Laboratory about New Visualities and Documentary Strategies amid Growing Ecological and Political Anxieties*, edited by Geocinema and Freeport, 33–5. Freeport.

Trinh, T. Minh-ha. 1991. *When the Moon Waxes Red: Representation, Gender, and Cultural Politics*. New York: Routledge.

XqSu. 2021. "Dust Storms, Green Waves. A Lattice of Violent, Global Relations Sustains China's Colonization of 'Xinjiang.'" *Lausan. Hk.* Accessed June 30, 2022. https://lausan.hk/2021/dust-storms-green-waves.

XqSu. 2022. "Overland There's Shorter Time to Dream." In *Deserts Are Not Empty*, edited by Samia Henni, 210–59. New York, NY: Columbia University Press.

Media Infrastructures, Geopolitics and Colonization of the Deep Sea

Armin Linke in conversation with Petra Löffler

Armin Linke's long-term artistic research on the discursive construction of the seabed sheds light on legal, scientific as well as visual registers that intersect in the ongoing debate on resource extraction and the juridical status of the ocean's floor. In his multichannel video installation *Prospecting Ocean* Linke focuses on images as operational tools of marine science and material witnesses that function as evidence for the legal decisions of the International Seabed Authority. Thereby he interrogates the crossing of power relations, media infrastructures, and neo-colonial practices of extraction. But *Prospecting Ocean* also displays the tension between legal frameworks, state authorities, and protests in Papua New Guinea against the exploitation of the seabed and its harmful social, economic, and environmental consequences. The conversation turns to this tension and reflects on the role of complex technical apparatuses in the form of remotely controlled vehicles that float between visual knowledge production and the mapping and extracting of natural resources on the seabed.

Keywords: Media Infrastructure, Operational Image, Cartography, Artistic Research, Climate Change, Deep-sea Mining, Extraction, Law of the Sea, Environmental Activism

117

Petra Löffler: Armin, as artist and researcher you are interested in the interdependence of nature, culture, and technology—especially how the material environment in which humans and other species are living and is shaped by technologies and practices that are interconnected and respond to each other. In your artistic practice you focus on how humans thereby inform and produce, construct and transform infrastructure. Already in 2017 your exhibition *Oceans—Dialogues Between Ocean Floor and Water Column* was presented at the Edith-Russ-Haus für Medienkunst in Oldenburg. I would especially like to discuss how your multichannel video installation *Prospecting Ocean* relates to media infrastructures and anthropogenic climate change.[1] Produced by TBA21-Academy and shown for the first time during the Venice Architecture Biennale in 2018 as part of a large-scale solo exhibition, the installation was the result of your three-year artistic research project on the geopolitical and postcolonial issues of deep-sea mining and the current ecological challenges of protecting oceans against increasing economic exploitation and environmental degradation.

For this you combined footage from the deep sea, captured by remotely operated cameras, with documentary recordings of scientific labs, assemblies of the International Seabed Authority (ISA), and interviews with political decision makers, scientists, experts, and political activists around the world. The images from the deep sea were taken by cameras on remotely operated vehicles (ROVs), which are also used by mining companies to explore and extract what they expect to be economically profitable resources: metals such as copper and gold, polymetallic nodules, and minerals such as sulfur. These images not only represent a world that is usually hidden, but are a substantial part of the extractive practices and media technologies developed in the Global North. These produce visibility not only to increase knowledge, but to get into procession and to explore what was discovered by using these hegemonic practices and technologies. How do you consider the role of these advanced imaging technologies for the marine scientists you cooperated with in the project, as well as for your own artistic research and work?

Armin Linke: Yes, the exhibition started at Edith-Russ-Haus and then traveled to Venice, but before that we participated in a transdisciplinary project funded by the German Ministry for Education and Research, through which we got access to the archives of state funded scientific institutions, for example GEOMAR and MARUM.[2] For the video installation I used footage from their immense archives (→ 1).[3] What was interesting

1   Linke's works have been shown, for instance, at the Centre Pompidou in Paris, at the ZKM in Karlsruhe, and at the HKW in Berlin.

2   GEOMAR is the name of the Helmholtz Center for Marine Sciences located in Kiel. MARUM is the Research Center for Marine Environmental Sciences of Bremen University in collaboration with other marine research institutes in Northern Germany.

3   The project was realized in collaboration with Giulia Bruno (camera, editing), Giuseppe Ielasi (sound, editing), Renato Rinaldi (sound), and Kati Simon (project management). Sarah Kaehlert and Nils Strackbein from GEOMAR and MARUM gave support with the ROV Video Archive. See https://www.edith-russ-haus.de/no_cache/ausstellungen/ausstellungen/archiv.html?tx_kdvzerhapplications_pi4%5Bexhibition%5D=223&tx_kdvzerhapplications_pi4%5Baction%5D=show&tx_kdvzerhapplications_pi4%5Bcontroller%5D=Exhibition (accessed August 9, 2022).

for us as artists was not so much how the complex processes of making science can be depicted, but more how science itself uses these images as a tool. At GEOMAR, MARUM, and other European marine science institutes we were looking at how exactly certain media technologies were used by the scientists and what kind of images they produced. Later in the development of the project with TBA21-Academy we also collaborated with other institutions like NTNU in Trondheim, Norway, where we were allowed to film training sessions for pilots of underwater remote-operated vehicles.

GEOMAR and MARUM are two of the world-leading institutions in imaging technologies. They collaborate with the research ship "Sonne" based at the University of Oldenburg.[4] The images are basically produced by the pilots to see where the rovers are going and are recorded for further scientific evaluation. They are used to coordinate the actions of the ROV's pilot, who is in direct contact with the captain of the research ship (→ 2). In fact, that's a very complicated coordination, and the whole ship with all its material as well as informational infrastructure reminded me of a huge film set. One can say that the images taken by the ROV have a specific aesthetic quality, but for the scientists they were mostly visual evidence, for instance when they encountered a new species for the first time.

4   The research ship "Sonne" has been used since 2014 to investigate climate change and marine resources, but also to protect marine ecosystems predominantly in the Indo-Pacific. See https://portal-forschungsschiffe.de/schiffe/sonne (accessed August 9, 2022).

2 3 Installation view of Armin Linke's exhibition *Prospecting Ocean*, at CNR-ISMAR, curated by Stefanie Hessler, commissioned and produced by TBA21-Academy, Venice Italy 2018 © Giulia Bruno

All the footage taken by the ROV was stored in servers. I asked for permission to enter the server room and spent a week there looking at this vast image material. Together with musician Giuseppe Ielasi and artist Giulia Bruno I edited these, let's say, operational images,[5] more in a choreographic and aesthetic way. We also added sound using a random composition by John Cage and finally presented these operational images as a kind of panorama of the submarine landscapes in one section of the installation.

At the same time, we asked ourselves how to make the political implications of these operational images visible. By reading the logbooks of each ship campaign I figured out: What was the campaign about? What happened every day? I was also able to reconstruct who financed the trip, and what the particular purpose was. These findings we presented at the exhibition on a separate screen that in a certain way functioned as a guide for a geopolitical reading of the campaigns – that is, who was doing the recordings and for which scientific reason these operational, but nevertheless very aesthetic images were produced. Simply speaking, it was like looking backstage at a Hollywood film set and opening the production books. In the installation at the Istituto delle Scienze Marine (ISMAR) in Venice we tried to bring these, let's say, science-fiction technology images of the present in contact with other imaging and navigation technologies from earlier times. For this, we invited the local marine scientists to investigate the historical library of their own discipline, because geopolitical and infrastructural navigation tools have always played an important part in traversing, investigating, and colonizing the ocean (→3).

Petra: Your approach to the material and information infrastructure behind the research of marine scientists and the logistics necessary to conduct their operations sounds thrilling. I found the juxtaposition of images from various sources presented on different screens very meaningful in this respect. Would you please elaborate on the concept of the exhibition and what your intention was for the installation *Prospecting Ocean*?

Armin: The concept I developed together with Giulia Bruno and Giuseppe Ielasi, the graphic designer Linda van Deursen, and the exhibition architects Kuehn Malvezzi. The exhibition in Venice was curated by Stefanie Hessler and funded by the art foundation TBA21-Academy. We were very fortunate to collaborate with the local CNR-ISMAR Istituto di Scienze Marine, the oceanographic institute of Italy, for this occasion. The institute allowed us to exhibit in the laboratories of their abandoned

5   The term "operational image" or "operative image," coined by filmmaker Harun Farocki (2004) and media theorist Thomas Keenan (2004) among others, has been used to denounce automatically produced images for territory or transport surveillance that were strategically used by military forces or state authorities. A similar claim was made by Allan Sekula (1975) who used the term "instrumental image" analyzing military aerial photography.

old historical building on the Canal Grande, which was under re-construction or restauration at that time to be transformed into a cultural center and library. So, we didn't show the project in a classic exhibition space or museum, but in the very laboratory that was doing oceanographic research some years ago. In preparing the exhibition we investigated this special place and decided to present the artworks detached from the walls. The idea was that the artworks should not be simply hung on the walls and distributed over the rooms of the building, but that the institute and the building itself should be presented as an artwork, as a testimony of the scientific work that had taken place earlier in this building.

As you might know, the lagoon of Venice is in fact one of the very first artificial ecological systems in Europe. It was invented in the fifteenth century, diverting two rivers so that their sediment would not enter the lagoon, because this would have blocked the traffic then – the economic traffic but of course also the military defense system of the lagoon. Moreover, Venice was Europe's door to the old silk road, and the transportation of goods was only possible after the invention of cartography to visualize the lagoon's topography and the transportation infrastructure through the Mediterranean Sea into the lagoon. For this reason, it was interesting for us to show how the idea that the ocean is an infrastructure has evolved in a place that's historically very much connected to the same idea of changing the environment for economic purposes.

6   Davor Vidas is a research professor in international law and Director of the Law of the Sea Programme at the Fridtjof Nansen Institute, Lysaker, Norway. He is author of several articles and edited volumes on the history and contemporary challenges of the United Nations Convention on the Law of the Sea (UNCLOS); see Vidas, Zalasiewicz and Williams (2015) and Vidas and Freestone (2019).

7   The subtitle of Grotius's book, *The Right Which Belongs to the Dutch to Take Part in the East Indian Trade*, frankly expresses the geopolitical and economic interests of Dutch authorities and trading companies.

Speaking with the sea law specialist Davor Vidas,[6] who is also collaborating with scientists of the Anthropocene Working Group, I came across the book *Mare Liberum* (The Freedom of the Sea), published in 1609 by the Dutch lawyer Hugo Grotius, who was then only 32 years old. At that time European empires tried to colonize not only territories on the American continent, but also to bring shipping routes and marine resources under their rule. Grotius, who worked on behalf of the Dutch East India Company, which needed to reach their new colonies in Indonesia, contested the exclusive rights over eastern trading routes by the Portuguese and Spanish, claiming that the sea could not be owned by any state.[7] He finally convinced them and also the Pope to accept his concept of international waters, indicating that these areas are different from "terra firma" (dry land) and should be considered as international territory and thus be free for everybody, for every nation to traverse. This was the beginning of liberalism if you wish.

We asked ISMAR to give us one sediment core extracted from the lagoon of Venice in the 1950s, when the chemical industry was introduced into the region as part of the Marshall Plan development, obviously with high ecological risks. We wanted to know if one could find toxic chemicals in the sedimented layers representing the geological history of the lagoon. The industrialization created the severe problem of subsidence of the lagoon, because a lot of water was extracted by the local chemical industry in the first decades until 1972. As a result, the lagoon's subsidence is about five centimeters, and these are exactly the centimeters that we probably will lose with the possible next sea level rise.

We tried to visualize these different histories of the lagoon because you might think, as a European citizen, that geological exploitation of the sea floor is something very new and remote, but you can also find it much closer in the environmental history of the lagoon and the very place of the exhibition. The idea for the exhibition was for visitors to see different visualizations of the diverse histories of the ocean while walking through the historical offices of ISMAR: from the lagoon and its history to places like Papua New Guinea, where we filmed environmental activists in conflict with the first attempts of deep-sea mining in national waters. The installation had its focal point on the threats of deep-sea mining aiming to extract metals and minerals from the ocean, which are needed to produce phones and computers, but also batteries for electrical cars. The mining operations entail huge risks, which are mostly deliberately ignored by profit seeking companies.[8]

8   The influential oceanographer Sylvia A. Earle has been criticizing the risks of deep-sea mining for years now; see for instance her post "Deep Sea Mining: An Invisible Land Grab" (July 20, 2016). https://mission-blue.org/2016/07/deep-sea-mining-an-invisible-land-grab (accessed August 9, 2022).

To conclude, the basic idea of the installation was to present this diverse visual material not only in its aesthetic quality, but as important operational tools of our time that are used to exploit and profit from the resources of the deep sea and the seabed. At a tipping point for oceanic ecologists, *Prospecting Ocean* weaves an intricate network of advanced technology, extractive industry, marine science, geopolitics, and economics in the Global Norths as well as its effects on the nations of the Global South, at the new frontier of deep-sea aesthetics and geopolitics. In this network images and especially maps of different seabed areas play an important role, where scientific institutions as well as stakeholders tried to define, imagine, or map the deep sea to exploit its resources.

Petra: How did you manage to get access to those remote places where deep-sea mining projects started and to other places where the rights to do so were negotiated?

Armin: The first time I came to Papua New Guinea I wanted to visit some of the areas where deep-sea mining extraction was planned, but this was somehow complicated. I understood that much deeper research was necessary to identify the different stakeholders and engage with them. Later I found out by chance that the International Seabed Authority is based in Kingston, Jamaica. The task of this UN organization established in 1994 is to define how seabed resources in international waters should be shared between the different developed countries in the Global North and the Global South. I was attending the International Seabed Authority Twenty-Second Annual Session in 2016 where we were allowed to film a meeting of this organization and started to look at the legal material concerning the rights to exploit marine resources (→ 4). A section of the film for *Prospecting Ocean* is specifically on this issue. There we presented a plan that was already developed in the late 1960s to regulate the access to the seafloor: "When, in the 1960s, it became known that in the deep seabed of the open sea there might be huge metal and mineral resources beyond national jurisdiction, fused into so-called polymetallic nodules, the question was who should profit from those resources – the developed wealthier countries of the Global North who have the technologies to exploit those resources or the developing poorer countries of the Global South who need the money from deep-sea mining? In 1967, the ambassador of Malta, which had just become independent from the United Kingdom three years before, proposed that everything beyond national jurisdiction should be the common heritage of humankind, thereby referring to Grotius's formulation of a sea convention from the seventeenth century."[9]

9   Excerpt taken from Armin Linke *Prospecting Ocean* (2018) referring to Maltese ambassador Arvid Pardo, one of the founders of the common heritage of humankind concept under international law who received the Third World Prize in 1983. In 1982 the United Nations Convention on the Law of the Sea (UNCLOS) was inaugurated.

Technologies like the sonar to map and investigate the seabed were already developed during the Second World War and even more with submarine warfare during the Cold War, so a new cartography of the sea floor was available. This is to say, the discovery of new mineral resources was possible through this new cartographic imaging technology. To share the discovered resources of minerals in the seabed between industrialized and developing countries, a new set of laws was introduced at the same time when the so-called Moon Treaty of 1979 was introduced for exploring the moon, which was considered a shared human resource as well. We conducted interviews on the history of these legal instruments and documents and asked ourselves how legal infrastructure is installed. I was allowed to film the meetings of the International Seabed Authority in Kingston in the setting of its modernistic architecture and its symbolic language. In the '90s it was regarded as important to have an institution of the United Nations in a developing country and not only in New York or Geneva. The architects tried to incorporate signs of the local tradition into

4   International Seabed Authority (ISA), Twenty-Second Session of the International Seabed
    Authority, Kingston, Jamaica 2016 © Armin Linke

5   International Seabed Authority (ISA), manganese nodule, Kingston, Jamaica 2016
    © Armin Linke

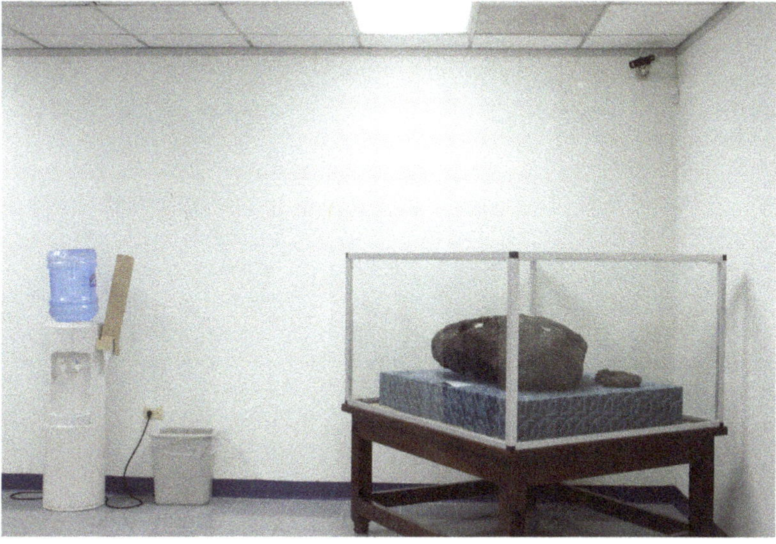

the materials and details of the modernistic building. The ISA building houses very interesting displays as for example large polymetallic nodules in front of the coffee shop or photos of rare deep-sea creatures along its corridors or maps of the submarine cable system that is also regulated by the ISA (→5).

Petra: We started our conversation with thinking about the role of infrastructure for climate change, and how climate change affects infrastructures and the parameters of their development. As you argue, exploring the ocean is a true challenge regarding the different interests of marine scientists, legal authorities, industrial stakeholders, and mining companies. To go on with an obvious question: To what degree or in what respect can the ocean itself be considered an infrastructure? Or to put it differently: What kind of infrastructure is the ocean?

Armin: In the exhibition we wanted to show how the development of infrastructure relates to legal structures and decisions. At the Walther Schücking Institute for International Law in Kiel I did an interview with Erik van Doorn.[10] This institute is an official repository of copies of all legal documents produced by the UN on the topic of international sea law.[11] He and other colleagues are working on the legal aspects of the oceans. His research deals with the legal implications on the common habitat in principle for highly migratory fish stocks. This is interesting because the same legal sets can be applied to living beings such as fish and other marine species as well as to stones and other non-living material. All these resources have a legal set that can be translated from one to the other.

Polymetallic nodules are quite mysterious because it's not clear how they evolve, or if there is an organic core. Somehow, they attract minerals and grow in time, and it takes millions of years to create them. The scientists at the Unit of Mineral Processing (AMR) at Aachen University, where the interview took place, are specialized in developing technologies to extract the minerals from these polymetallic nodules. What I learned from them is that the substances that make up the polymetallic nodules are very diffused, and it is rather difficult to raffinate them. Moreover, it is still—which is probably good—very expensive to do this, but scientists at the AMR are working on optimizing this process. You could say that biological diversity or biological life is now a new resource for which a new juridical infrastructure is needed.

Besides polymetallic nodules there are other resources such as black smokers that you can find on the seabed of the deep sea. They emit mostly methane gases and sulfur and therefore

10   Erik van Doorn is research associate at the GEOMAR institute in Kiel. Linke is referring to his dissertation *Legal implications of the common heritage principle for highly migratory fish stock* (2019) at the Institute for International Law at Kiel University.

11   The Walther Schücking Institute was founded in 1914 and deals specifically with international law. It houses Germany's largest and oldest university library specializing in international law as well as the UN Depository Library.

are very interesting for pharmaceutical industries. It was discovered that certain bacteria living in symbiosis with other animals like crabs can transform these lethal elements into sugar by a process called chemosynthesis. It is still not clear if these are living matter and fall under the assumption of the common heritage of mankind or if they are related to the geological rock sediments of the black smokers and thus fall under the United Nations Convention on the Law of the Sea (UNCLOS) legislation. Therefore, another set of legal infrastructure is needed today for the pharmaceutical industry to patent the molecular processes of these life forms. There arises a tension between the potential pharmaceutical investments and the mineral industry that wants to exploit the rare earth mineral sediments emitted by black smokers. Many marine biologists and international organizations have suggested introducing an extraction moratorium, as it would be important to learn about the potentials of these life forms before eradicating them or raising them for geological issues.[12]

12 At the 2022 UN Ocean Conference in Lisbon, the Pacific Island states of Palau and Fiji called for a moratorium on deep-sea mining. They demand that the International Seabed Authority (ISA) should not license any seabed mining for the time being because the mining industry must be prevented from irretrievably destroying deep-sea ecosystems and violating the human rights of Pacific islanders.
See https://un.org/en/conferences/ocean2022 (accessed August 17, 2022).

These legal negotiations have also far-reaching geopolitical consequences. From the seventeenth century onward the national seawater zone was only three nautical miles from the coast because that was the distance a cannon ball could reach. Today the exclusive economic zone under the rule of a state reaches out to about 200 nautical miles. But if a state can show that its continental shelves don't go down abruptly but smoothly, then the authorities can ask for an extension of the exclusive economic zone (EEZ) up to 350 nautical miles. That is, you can expand your territory further into the sea. This is a process that started about ten years ago. So all states showed up at the United Nations Commission on the Limits of the Continental Shelf (CLCS) with different visualizations and geological tools indicating how their continental shelf is going smoothly into the ocean to their own advantage. For Norway, for example, this is very interesting, because they will have even more oil fields and possibilities to exploit black smokers if they are allowed to expand their territory further. The same goes for Portugal and the Azores. This process of "colonization" that is happening at the moment could change the economy and the resources of some states completely.

Petra: I want to return to the question of how the ocean can be regarded as infrastructure. From your previous answer I learned that there are many different layers or infrastructural registers. You talked about the laws that regulate not only the ocean, but the seabed and the territory around the continental shelves. You also mentioned the economic interests of certain states to further expand the territory beyond their coastlines and into the open sea. And I suddenly remembered that even in the Mediterranean Sea there are conflicts between Turkey and Greece because their border runs between their many islands. The state to which even a small island belongs has the right to increase the territory around this island according to this new law, and this expanded territory can overlap with another neighboring island and its expanded territory, which belong to another state. That is one reason why Greece and Turkey are arguing about the jurisdiction of certain seabeds – and because both state authorities expect to find resources there.

Concerning these complex discussions about the expansion of territory and the international sea laws that regulate this expansion, it has become clear to me that this is also a geo-political question: When we regard the ocean and the seabed as infrastructure, who has the power to implement this infra-structure and who controls and has access to it? You talked about Papua New Guinea and the local people who could not profit from the developing of seabed mining because it is in the hand of international mining companies. This situation raises conflicts between international investors, mining companies, and state authorities who want to exploit this seemingly open space and local environmental activists who want to protect the ocean's biodiversity as a "natural" resource. That is, the ocean has become a highly contested space.

Armin: Yes, of course, the ocean is historically a geopolitically important space. And when we speak of the Mediterranean Sea, the issue is not only the submarine gas fields between Greece and Turkey. The two parts of Cyprus also have a con-tested gas field. There are increasingly more conflicts over these resources between states that claim territories in the Mediterranean Sea. These geopolitical issues are continuously happening, unfortunately often unnoticed by a wider public. For instance, parts of the Mediterranean logistical and economical infrastructures such as ports in Italy and Greece were bought by Chinese companies during the last financial crisis. There is a whole interchange of infrastructure, which is, again, a very pressing geopolitical issue.

Petra: When I started thinking about infrastructures, I was more concerned with media infrastructures because the deep sea is such a hidden space for most human observers.[13] You need equipment to go down there and especially technologies, for instance very strong flood lights because of the absence of light in the deep sea. You already talked about the remote-ly operated vehicle technology and about operative images, images that do something. This is especially the case with the

13   For a cultural history of the deep sea see Rozwadowski (2008) and Ada-mowsky (2016).

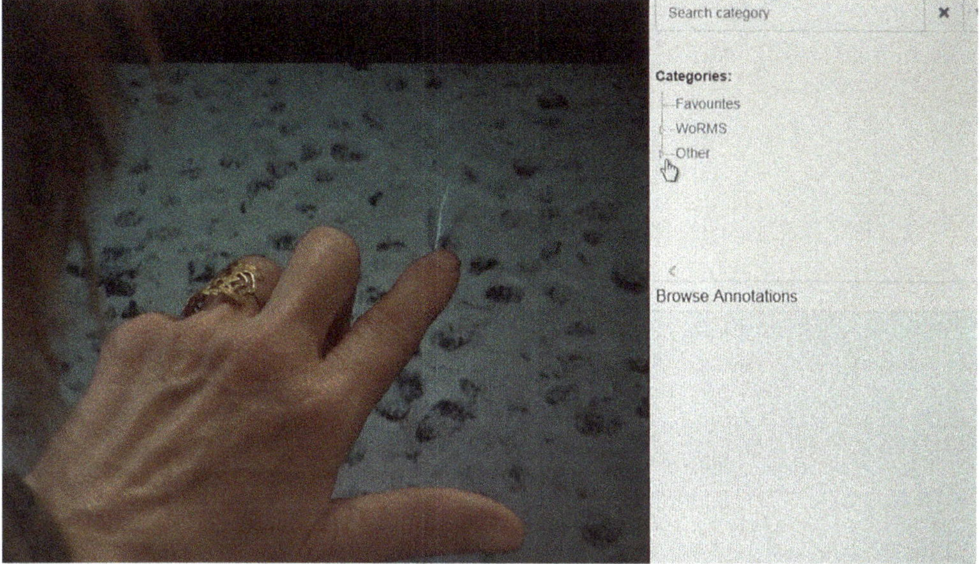

14   Sociologist of science Janet Vertesi (2015) has explained how scientists from NASA's Mars Exploration Rover Team produced images for mapping the planet.

15   Ann Vanreusel is an expert in deep-sea benthos and head of the research group Marine Biology at Ghent University, which has participated in international research projects and networks. Recently she investigated the impact of climate change on polar systems, the acidification of the sea, and the extraction of polymetallic nodules.

ROVs. You showed us a slide where a person was trained in operating the vehicle. What especially fascinates me is the fact that people in laboratories are doing things that have effects on far away regions, thousands of kilometers away – regions that they couldn't enter with their own senses. This is to say, they are operating from a distance and it's something you can only do with media. In *Prospecting Ocean*, you also used footage of a marine biologist, who pointed with her hand to the computer monitor, explaining something to you (→ 6). Media technologies are necessary to work on the seabed, as well as in outer space. ROVs are a sort of spaceship, if you wish, and there are indeed some similarities between approaching outer space and entering deep sea.[14] Can you explain what you experienced when you were talking with the scientists in the labs, about what they were doing and how they were approaching this far away space, having the impression that they're closer than they in fact are?

Armin: Ann Vanreusel, a marine biologist that I met at the International Seabed Authority meeting and visited for an interview at the Marine Biology Research Group at Ghent University[15] explained to me how the ROV technology changes the way marine scientists work: "We don't know what is there and it's a big task to get an idea of the biodiversity there. When I started to work at ROVs I was, on one hand, amazed to see what we could do, because all of a sudden we were working in a submarine environment of a depth of 4000 or 5000 meters… I mean, we were seeing what we were doing. Before that we were working in the deep sea blind, actually by lowering reps from a ship. Now you would walk on seabed like you would walk on a beach, but still, you see, it's not perfect because you have these arms, and you need to collect these very tiny, delicate specimens. And so, what happened here is just that the sponge was collected and then you lost it again...and also, how much time it takes to collect one specimen, one little sponge. And so, while there are thousands of sponges, I mean, you have two pilots that are driving, that need to keep the ROV in place and they need to steer the arms to collect this tiny sponge with a stalk as fine as a needle. So here he grabbed it again. So the trick is to get it here on the shelf and you see the shelf is being opened. And so, to get it in the box and then it can be brought up. So, it's nearly a million-dollar sponge."[16]

16 Excerpt taken from Armin Linke *Prospecting Ocean* (2018).

I really like the idea of a million-dollar sponge!

A highly equipped research ship like "Sonne" is connected to and localized via the GPS satellites together with a network of buoys that send sonar signals. All these signals create a network around the ship that makes it possible to localize the ROV underwater. The two pilots of the ROV are in continuous contact with the captain of the ship. One pilot takes care of the vehicle, which is connected to the main ship, like a child connected to its mother by an umbilical cord, and everyone is afraid that it will strangle itself. The other pilot takes care of the operational robotic arms to collect geological samples and living creatures. Now you can imagine how expensive one hour of navigation with the ROV in fact is. Therefore, often the ROV's navigation time is shared between different scientists. It might be that there is a group of geologists and a group of biologists. And of course, maybe their attitude about conservation is different, but anyhow, they share the same ROV, the same time. It was explained to me that if there are more scientists on the ship, there is always, for each day, one scientist who is the spokesman of the scientists to the pilots. So, a scientist cannot speak directly to the pilots "Oh, there is an interesting plant, go there!" Instead, the scientists need to discuss and decide their priorities and then the spokesman should speak to the pilots: "How do we use the next half an hour? Or what should we do if the main ship is in a storm, but for the ROV that's not so important?" There are a lot of issues and complications that the collective must decide on. I became aware that it is an issue of negotiation between the pilots and the scientists and the situation that they paid for this ROV time.

What is also important concerning the ROV's imaging technology is that there is only one camera to operate in a three-dimensional space. When the pilots use the arm, trying to grab for instance a certain sponge, they only see through the lens of the camera, which makes the task more difficult. I have the impression that some of the scientists live in a contradiction, and they are aware of it, because on one side they want to keep the seabed intact. On the other side the equipment for the research is so sophisticated and expensive that they need to collaborate with the companies. The scientific and ecological research provides and sets the data from which the industry can develop proposals to begin mining at a particular site. It is the political body and its institutions like the ISA that set the rules for interpreting these assessments. So, the work of the scientists has a highly political value.

Petra: It has become clear now, at least for me, that especially the deep sea has become a very complex underwater infrastructure that is vulnerable and needs a lot of human expertise and continuous maintenance work. Moreover, the decisions of the researchers are important in respect to how this material marine infrastructure, as well as media technologies that make the exploration possible in the first place, are used and how their use affects the environment.

Armin: There is more to say about the history of imaging technologies concerning the mapping of the sea. The research done by Marie Tharp in the mid twentieth century is an interesting case in this respect. Starting in 1948 she worked as a trained geologist at the Lamont-Doherty Earth Observatory of Columbia University in New York, where she, together with her partner Bruce C. Heezen, developed a method to exactly map the then mostly uninvestigated seabed. She developed the idea of using sonar technology to get data from the different heights and depths of the ocean floor. At that time, she, as a woman, was not allowed to go on the ship to supervise the soundings. With the recordings by the sonar, she began to work on a continuous representation of the seabed by making manual calculations and created a very precise map of the North Atlantic ocean's floor from these data. She published her findings first in 1959 as *The Floors of the Oceans* together with Maurice Ewing and Bruce C. Heezen, who is better known than Tharp maybe because he put his name on most of the papers they published together.

However, her discovery of the rift valley along the Mid-Atlantic Ridge, of which she gave a more accurate representation, was very influential for the acceptance of the theories of plate tectonics and continental drift, which were confirmed in the 1950s and '60s through sonar technology. Moreover, Tharp and Heezen went to Innsbruck to meet the landscape painter

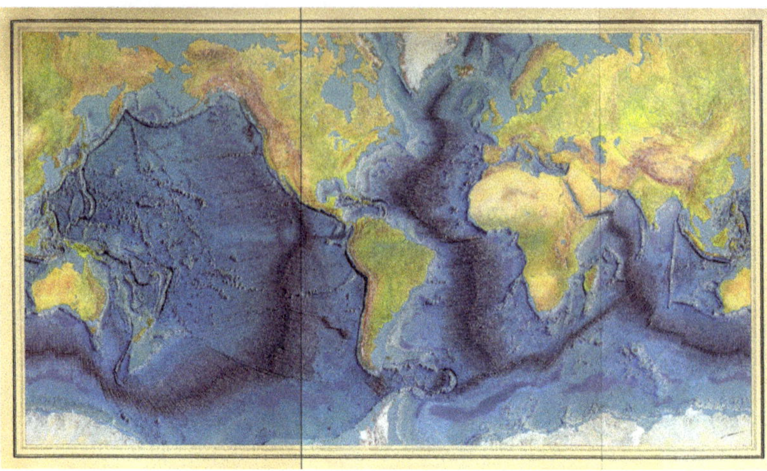

and illustrator Heinrich C. Berann who created very illustrative
maps of Alpine landscapes. He agreed to make a map of the
entire world ocean floor to be presented at the United Nations
(→ 7). This is also a case where technology, science, and art
meet and their singular histories are entangled.

Petra: Concerning the importance of maps for having an image
of the world, it is convincing to argue that different maps can
change one's perspective on that world, especially regarding
the quantity of space occupied by the sea. That becomes obvious when looking at a globe on which not the continents are
highlighted but the oceans between them. In fact, it's a change
of perspective when you regard the oceans as a huge space
covering the seabed which is a territory of its own with moun-
tains and valleys.

But coming back to your work as an artist and researcher – and
I underline the term artist here – what aesthetic decisions did
you make in selecting and arranging the film material? Watching
Prospecting Ocean one can get an impression of how closely
you work with the marine scientists, looking over their shoul-
ders almost all the time. But in the end, you are the one who
decides on the arrangement of the images for the installation
on different screens. In other words: What form of evidence can
your artwork generate regarding the concerns of prospecting
oceans and the negotiating of conflicts about exploiting the
seabed? What was your intention behind this project?

Armin: To answer your question I want to underline first that I
worked on this project together with the musicians Giuseppe

Ielasi and Renato Rinaldi and with the artist and biologist Giulia Bruno – so we were not a classical film team. Thanks to TBA21-Academy, which commissioned the project, we were the first artists allowed to film at the International Seabed Authority. Starting from this event over the three years of production we formed a network of lawyers, scientists, activists, and institutions with which we communicated to develop the research and the installation.

So, your question is: How can a project conducted by artists like this reach its audience and influence public opinion about current ecological issues? Our idea was not to set these images together and to explain them to the public like in a common TV documentary, but to edit continuously from one image to another, from one place to another, to places that don't seem to be connected, making the viewer ask: What does a university in Norway have to do with a meeting at the United Nations in New York or a legal meeting in South Africa with an activist group in Papua New Guinea? By making these connections I ask the audience to imagine the connection. My work is not really documentary in the sense that it rather poses questions and asks the audience to be curious, to become active and research these questions by themselves. And of course, I think that the film works even better in the context of the installation, or when you read the texts by Stefanie Hessler.[17] If you wish, the exhibition works like a footnote to the film and as a moment of activation.

For my recent project at Haus der Kulturen der Welt (HKW) in Berlin I again collaborated with different groups of local activists in the Bismarck Ramu Group and in Papua New Guinea.[18] I was allowed to film a meeting of a think tank of the German Ministry for the Environment, Nature Conservation, Nuclear Safety and Consumer Protection. They organized this meeting for different stakeholders, representatives from German companies that are developing technologies that could potentially be used in deep-sea mining, with the participation of activists or ecologists.

Petra: Papua New Guinea was partly a German colony in the Pacific until 1914...

Armin: Exactly. If you visit the Ethnological Museum at the Humboldt Forum in Berlin, you will find a whole section dedicated to this area, because the German colonizers brought a lot of artifacts from there. When we traveled around the Bismarck Sea, we anchored at Finschhafen, where we visited a refinery for batteries on the coast. All the byproducts are just

---

17　Hessler (2019) refers with the title and many times throughout her book to Linke's *Prospecting Ocean* which she connects to other artworks and a great variety of sources from cultural and media history, philosophy, feminist theory and natural sciences. Her book, which also includes a visual essay by Armin Linke, inspired this conversation with the artist.

18　The exhibition *Earth Indices: Processing the Anthropocene*, realized together with Giulia Bruno, took place from May to October 2022.

19   The Solwara 1
Seafloor Massive Sul-
fide (SMS) prospect
located in the Bis-
marck Sea some 35
nautical miles north
of Rabaul contains a
substantial resource
of massive base met-
al sulfides, gold and
silver. Solwara means
in the local Tok Pisin
language "saltwater"
synonymous with
"sea." The company
collapsed 2019 due
to financial problems.

dumped into the sea, creating an incredible ecological disaster. Later we went to the New Ireland province of Papua New Guinea. The area between Rabaul on New Britannia and the small island Niolam is where the former Canadian-Australian company Nautilus Minerals Inc. started the world's first deep-sea mining project in 2010 called "Solwara 1," 1,700 meters below seawater level.[19] At that time, the Canadian-Australian-based company, financed among others by a Russian investment group, was developing its technology and ships in China. Of course, deep-sea mining in international waters is still not permitted. But what is permitted are prospects to find resources for future exploitation. However, ecological standards of deep-sea mining have not been developed yet. But somehow this company arranged with the central government of Papua New Guinea and got permission to do prospections in that region in national waters. This sparked conflicts with the local people, their traditional way of life, and rituals that are still very influential on a local basis today. You must imagine that they speak around 820 languages, so nearly each village has its own language. It's an incredibly sophisticated culture, but also a very regional and local one, which means there are often problems between central and local governments. Finally, the local government denied deep-sea mining. Consequently, the mining company moved to a remote island and planned to start mining there because the inhabitants did not have easy access to information infrastructure (cellphone networks and mobile internet) to communicate and organize themselves against the mining.

20   The island group
belonged from 1884
to 1919 to the Ger-
man colonies in the
Pacific.

First, when we arrived on the coral islands of Atafu formerly known as the Duke of York Group,[20] we only wanted to make a documentation, but soon we realized that by providing fuel for boats and generators to produce electricity, so that people could recharge their cell phones, we became part of their activities and learned about their concerns and constraints. At the same day on the small Ramoaina Island a municipality meeting was held where the whole village came together. We also went there and started filming the meeting. When the people began to speak about deep-sea mining, we participated in the discussion about how they could organize (→8). As a matter of fact, deep-sea mining would endanger the fishing grounds, which is often the main or only resource the islanders have to earn a living. And due to the rise in sea level, which is already very evident, agriculture is endangered, too. Consequently, local people are very skeptical about deep-sea mining, since only the companies from the Global North will profit from it. That is why I really liked what Jenny said about this issue at the community meeting that we were filming: "You know what,

I'm also a company. You teach me how to be a capitalist. Now I have a bank account, so I have a financial infrastructure. So, I have a company and why has my company less rights than the other company?"[21] In our film we wanted to give a voice to these people who are often not being heard by authorities and people from the Global North. You can say the sea has an incredible cultural history and a very rich mythology in many cultures, not only in the Global North.

Petra: It seems to me that the community meeting you included in the film is an example of the self-activating local use of global information infrastructures. I'm very grateful that you have turned to this issue, bringing together the challenges of anthropogenic climate change and capitalist economies, exploitation of resources and coloniality, material and information infrastructures. And this is only one instance where it becomes evident that the question of who is prospecting the ocean for what purposes has consequences far beyond legal infrastructures or resource extraction. The different geopolitical interests and conflicts concerning deep-sea mining are also connected to colonial pasts and presences including various cultural histories, Indigenous epistemologies and local mythologies in the Pacific Island region or Oceania.[22]

21   Excerpt taken from Armin Linke *Prospecting Ocean* (2018).

22   These questions have been addressed by local activists and scientists who participate in discussions evolving around climate change and insist on the relevance of Indigenous knowledge systems to establish sustainable relations to the ocean and its many islands (see Koya Vaka'uta, Vaka'uta and Lagi 2018).

Adamowsky, Natascha. 2016. *The Mysterious Science of the Sea, 1743–1954*. New York, NY/London: Routledge.

Farocki, Harun. 2004. "Phantom Images." *Public* 29: 12–22.

Hessler, Stefanie. 2019. *Prospecting Ocean*. Cambridge, MA/London: MIT Press.

Keenan, Tom. 2004. "Light Weapons." In *Harun Farocki: Working on the Sightlines*, edited by Thomas Elsaesser, 203–10. Amsterdam: Amsterdam University Press.

Koya Vaka'uta, Cresantia Frances, Lingikoni Vaka'uta, and Rosiana Lagi. 2018. "Reflections from Oceana on Indigenous Epistemology, the Ocean, and Sustainability." In *Tidalectics. Imagining an Oceanic Worldview Through Art and Science*, edited by Stefanie Hessler, 127–31. Cambridge, MA/London: MIT Press.

Rozwadowski, Helen. 2008. *Fathoming the Ocean: The Discovery and Exploration of the Deep Sea*. Cambrigde, MA: Belknap Press of Harvard University Press.

Sekula, Allan. 1975. "The Instrumental Image: Steichen at War." *Artforum* 14 (4): 26–35.

Vertesi, Janet. 2015. *Seeing Like a Rover: How Robots, Teams, and Images Craft Knowledge of Mars*. Chicago, IL/London: University of Chicago Press.

Vidas, Davor, Jan Zalasiewicz and Mark Williams. 2015. "What is the Anthropocene and Why is it Important for the Law." *Yearbook of International Environmental Law* 25 (1): 3–23.

Vidas, Davor and David Freestone. 2019. *International Law and Sea Level Rise. Report of the International Law Association Committee on International Law and Sea Level Rise*. Leiden/Boston, MA: Brill.

Cultivating Affect: Reparative Readings against Climate Change's *White* Sentiment

Katrin Köppert

This contribution explores the question of why it so difficult to connect affectively with climate change and what role the visual politics of anesthetization play in this. The focus is first on Elon Musk's laughter as an acting out of a *white* sentiment of insusceptibility and ignorance, before turning to the photographs of Sammy Baloji and David Shongo to discuss aestheticization as metallurgical, material, and, thus, an intense touch that is reparative insofar as it helps to affectively recognize and acknowledge anthropogenic climate change in its colonial, unevenly distributed extent of destruction without mobilizing the utopian potential of wanting to restore nature or landscape to a pristine state, since this idea of nature is a modern/colonial project again. Thus, the cultivation of affect aims at a decolonial ecology where nature is understood as interrelated and reciprocal, so that you take care of it while it takes care of you.

Keywords: *White* Sentiment, Black Affect, Climate Change, Extraction, Cobalt, Silver, Photography, Reparative Reading, Patching, Touching Images

Recently I reread philosopher Brian Massumi's text *The Future Birth of the Affective Fact* (2010). Throughout the reading, I was preoccupied with the question of how it is possible that his proposition of the affective facticity of threat is in no way applicable to anthropogenic climate change or the political and discursive consequences that should result from climate change.

The foil against which Massumi argued at the time was 9/11 and the subsequent "war on terror," stretching basically to the withdrawal of U.S. troops from Afghanistan in 2021. His argument in 2010 was that the threat of a new attack in the future would be felt in the present and considered real in that present. The war on terror was thus based on a fact of threat that was merely affective. The most telling example of this was Bush's war against Iraq, based purely on the pretextual assumption that it had nuclear weapons.

With anthropogenic climate change it seems to be the opposite: the threat, which after all is real not only in the future but already now, seems to be transformed into a reduction, even negation of affectivity that results in a refusal to sustainably change one's own behavior or to forcefully demand changes from politics. Whereas at the time an affective relationship was established with the unlikely possibility of a repeated terrorist attack, today the denial of affect seems to dominate with regard to the very high probability of catastrophes caused by climate change, so that climate policy remains in stagnation. Does the threat, then, have to be fictionalized before we can emotionally acknowledge it as real? Or, to put it another way, why might we be affectively attached to the status quo of fossil-fuel capitalism rather than to the threat it poses? Why is it that, for example, the majority of German citizens still cannot detach themselves from the car? Why is it that at the moment when we finally realize, due to the current war in Ukraine, that we have to do without oil and gas, nuclear power is being called upon again by the German government as a solution option instead of renewable energy? The answers to these questions hold different truths and certainly need to be contextualized and situated. Thus, though this article takes as its starting point very broad questions, it will be narrowed down to not only a concrete example and geopolitical location, but also to a localized reparative reading as a critical practice that confronts cultivated politics of insusceptibility. The occasion for this article, although organized the other way around, are therefore specifically two photographic works of Sammy Baloji and David Shongo whose aesthetic procedures I consider reparative readings, not so much in the sense of hermeneutics, but as semiotic-material practices of care.

Cultivated Insusceptibility

One possible answer to the question of why we are stuck in denial is certainly that of the philosopher Alexis Shotwell (2022). She argues that the reason for our immobility is our complicity in everything that causes climate change. The impossibility of an innocent position keeps us in the lane of doing nothing. I can understand the argument, especially insofar as Shotwell means that right-wing actors try to put pressure on left-wing actors with the accusation of being complicitly entangled, so that the latter give up, overwhelmed by their moral obligation. And yet – I would like to claim – there is something missing in this reasoning. For it presupposes that we feel guilty in the first place and are affectively connected to the consequences. That this presupposition is not at all self-evident is addressed by anthropologist Tamar Blickstein (2019) in her research on colonial affects in the realm of environmental racism. She emphasizes that Black people, Indigenous people, People of Color are disproportionately affected by the effects of climate change economically, but also viscerally and emotionally due to health complaints. But she also shows the extent to which, for example, *white* settlers affectively relate so strongly to their tradition of "firsting" that the destruction of forests, for example, is less severe. Guilt or insight into their complicity do not seem to matter at all. On the contrary, it is the affective reference to a system of *white* supremacy that makes it possible to not couple affectively with climate change. Following the Americanist Xine Yao (2021), it could be said that the reference to settler sentiment cultivates insensitivity to climate change, but also to those most likely to be affected by it. That is, and geographer Kathryn Yusoff in reference to Saidiya V. Hartman (1997, 11) puts it this way: unresponsiveness or affective silence are cultivated, normalizing extraction, deforestation, and pollution. The affective framing, then, is not disaster. At least for some of us since the "'cultivated silence' about the normalcy of those extractive modes as deracialized" (Yusoff 2018, 4) has a non-disastrous quality only for the unmarked norm.

In a nutshell, this means two things: 1) *white* sentiment is an important factor in colonial dispossession, and 2) affects of those most likely to be affected by dispossession and anthropogenic climate change are derealized. Black feelings are anchored in their unthinkability due to "the onto-epistemological framework that structures civil society and the modern field of representation" (Palmer 2017, 32).

Anaestheticization – Visual Tactics of *White* Sentiment

What is crucial to the cultivated insusceptibility is, among other things, the visual politics of anesthetization, which in terms of visual and art history can be traced back to the end of the nineteenth century. Art historian Nicholas Mirzoeff (2014) describes how, at the height of industrialization, smog and coal mining technologies became part of landscape paintings of cities such as London or Paris, without detracting from the beauty and grandeur of the image.

Stylistic devices, such as the slightly elevated perspective from which scenes of pollution were depicted, enabled an aestheticization that functioned selectively because "imperial smog" (2014, 226) was seen as a positive sign of the vitality of the modern metropolis. The historical anaestheticization through stylistic devices of the sublime that rendered metropolitan pollution harmless still carries over into contemporary imagery so that extraction can be affectively legitimized. We see mine landscapes whose excavation seems natural and at times beautiful, which, as the new concept of climate disaster porn, also means to contemplatively enjoy "decorative features of decay" (Fay 2022, 41). At the very least those landscapes seem controllable. In this sense, art historian and critic T.J. Demos discusses aerial and satellite photographs of mines that document damage but always serve to give viewers a sense of control over what they are seeing (2017, 28).

Taking a somewhat different example of this anaesthetization as a starting point, I would like to address the question of which visual politics can be of help to arrive at a cultivation of affect that helps to emotionally acknowledge the Anthropocene in its unequally distributed extent of destruction without mobilizing the utopian potential of wanting to restore nature or landscape to a pristine state, since this idea of nature is a modern/colonial project again. Thus, the cultivation of affect aims to a decolonial ecology where nature is understood as interrelated and reciprocal, so that you take care of it while it takes care of you (Rodríguez Aguilera 2021, 52).

LOL – Laughing out Loud

Was it only a coincidence that the ceremonial staging of the opening of Tesla's Gigafactory in Grünheide near Berlin makes the car, in front of which the company's founder Elon Musk and chancellor of Germany Olaf Scholz are standing, appear as a zebra? I can only speculate about that. And yet the zebra look of the car establishes a connection that welds the conditions of electric mobility production with the colonial revisionist imaginaries of the safari adventurer.

The entanglement of electromobility in the colonial conditions of what is being described as Anthropocene disappear

1   Dietmar Woidke, Olaf Scholz and Elon Musk at the opening of the Tesla factory.
    (Source: DPA, 2022)
2   A soldier of the "Schutztruppe" in what was then German East Africa.
    (Source: Bundesarchiv, image 105-DOA6103, photo: Walther Dobbertin)

behind a staging that transforms the car production line into an entertainment show. The violence associated with the exploitation of landscape and people are laughed away in the visual discourse of this entertaining stunt. Elon Musk's laughter, when asked in 2021 if the Tesla plant would accelerate the water shortage in the province of Brandenburg (rnd 2021), can be understood as an echo of his father, who in 2018 told an entertaining adventure story about how he came to an emerald mine in Zambia like a child to a bath (de Wet 2018). I thus understand laughing away and laughter in this context as constitutive of the cultivation of silence in the face of devastating transformations. To laugh is to purge oneself of the political implications of one's actions. Humor, thus, seems to be a cover affect to the *white* sentiment of emotionally keeping away from the colonial and ecological disaster haunting the present.

The Musk family, who came from South Africa, owned an emerald mine in Zambia, a state bordering the Democratic Republic of Congo. Congo is the source – as of 2016 – of 60% of the cobalt used in the production of lithium-ion batteries. They find their biggest market in e-cars. When, at an earlier appearance in Grünheide, Musk could hardly contain himself with laughter in response to Armin Laschet's remark that hydrogen, too, could be the future of clean mobility, and retorted that everything, except electric mobility, is a waste of time, he was laughing at the expense of the children, who work in the mines, and to the detriment of the ruined landscapes. Laughter derealizes the Black bodies and postcolonial landscapes of Congo as material and affective witnesses to the Anthropocene. It affectively holds in invisibility the infrastructures that become noticeable as fragile and endangered under the pressure of change.

I wonder what visual discourses might be used, as a consequence of this sentiment of *white* supremacy, to react to the derealization – not least in order to be able to affectively connect as a *white* situated person with the colonial disaster that stands behind electromobility without just ending up in the shock rigidity of one's own inaction. This, as I would like to show, cannot be about switching from laughter as a mode of insensitivity to that of dramatization, as we experience with the image politics of climate change in the form of weather maps colored deep red. I see such an image politics as a visual translation of paranoia, which is often only magnified in the course of its critique. In this vein, gender and queer theorist Eve Kosofsky Sedgwick problematizes that critique which, in attempting to avoid negative affects such as paranoia and fear, leads to a concentration on exactly these negative affects (Sedgwick 2003). Magnifying affects under the burning glass of criticism creates relieving satisfaction as much as laughter, but does not necessarily lead to a political framework of transformation.

This political frame is made possible by two artistic positions to which I will now turn, without thereby wanting to outsource the processing of reparative readings to art and artists. The point will be to understand these proposals as artistic practices that do not contradict the decolonial activism of, for example, Indigenous groups, which, as Blickstein (2019, 161) alludes to, consider affects and emotional attachments to material resources such as forests and water as not external to political struggles. At the same time, we face the challenge of locating and making visible these points of connection to the visual activism of art even within the infrastructurization of electromobility and digitality, to magnify them microscopically in the present. The question either way is which notion of a critique of *white* ignorance we are dealing with, to what extent the approach of reparative reading redeems itself here, and what, if anything, is thereby transformed for a perspectivization of repair in favor of affect cultivated as receptivity.

Reparative Reading I: Patching
The artists Sammy Baloji and David Shongo are connected not only by the Democratic Republic of Congo, but also by the city of Lubumbashi. Both are by birth or living close-knit to this city, the second largest in the republic, which was built as a mining town for the sake of extraction by Belgian colonial masters in 1910 and was long dominated by copper mining. After the end of the Cold War and the waning strategic interest in uranium, which the Democratic Republic of Congo also had, the mining sector experienced a slump before being rediscovered in the wake of the mining of cobalt and other ores for the infrastructures of digitality and electromobility. The only difference this time being that the mines are now managed – sometimes self-dug – in a decentralized and deregulated, in short, neoliberal manner.

The photomontages of Sammy Baloji's *Memoire* series, dating from 2006, show the abandoned, sometimes dilapidated industrial facilities of Lubumbashi. These plants are the material witnesses of a disastrous present, a ruined time of the now. The abandoned mines and facilities form the extremely dangerous infrastructure of current cobalt mining. Much like the gold mines in South Africa that Rosalind Morris filmed for *The Gamblers: The Zama Zama Miners in South Africa* (2019),[1] they are at risk of collapse and represent toxic working environments.

1   For a discussion of the anthropological film project see Morris and Eschkötter (2019).

By applying black-and-white photographs showing the origins of colonial industrial activities in Katanga, the area where

5   Sammy Baloji: *Untitled #17. Mémoire series*, 2006. Archival digital photograph on satin matte paper, 23 3/5 × 63 in, Editions 3–10 of 10+1AP

6   Sammy Baloji: *Untitled #18. Mémoire series*, 2006. Archival digital photograph on satin matte paper, 23 3/5 × 63 in, Editions 4–10 of 10+1AP

Lubambashi is located, the ruined present collides with the past of colonialism, which has been the ruin to Black people and landscapes. Even before landscapes can be romanticized as ruins, they are framed in terms of colonial history by means of the appliquéd bodies of enslaved workers or, in following anthropological photography (Edwards 1992, Morton and Edwards 2017), taxonomically mapped Black people. To elaborate on the coloniality of power in the present, which is the colonial practices and legacies of European colonialism in social orders and forms of knowledge (Quijano 2016), Baloji draws on historical photographs in the discursive field of anthropology. Landscape can consequently be seen as a discursive and technological operation of photographic measurement and scalability related to measurement. The people depicted in the photographs, in turn, appear as extractable materiality due to the industrial landscapes surrounding them. According to Kathryn Yusoff, who discusses the racial implications of slavery and the colonial affinities between Blackness and geology, Blackness is expressed as a geological formation and can be exploited like a mine:

Another way to conceive this would be to understand Blackness as a historically constituted and institutionally enacted deformation in the formation of subjectivity, a deformation that presses an inhuman categorization and the inhuman earth into intimacy. (Yusoff 2018, xii)

In this semiotic intertwining of Blackness and geology, Baloji works against dematerialization. Additionally, photography itself can be seen as a material and metallurgical manifestation of colonial extraction. With the mining landscapes as the backdrop or environment for the historical photographs, we can understand the history of photography as a colonial media geology. Namely, silver had to be extracted and processed for the photochemical process. With the chemical compounds of silver salts, photography is materially intertwined with the coloniality of the mine. Using historical black-and-white photographs as material witnesses, we can thus glimpse the cobalt that is in turn essential to the lenses and batteries of digital cameras.

The touch of the photographic surfaces, as staged by the layering of images, establishes the connection between extraction and photography, or rather, through the sensuality of this literal touch of surfaces, the materiality of photography is invoked in its entanglements with the colonial past and present. However, as I propose, this material touch simultaneously creates an intimacy that can be seen as reparative to the question of cultivating affect. In doing so, I would like to suggest the aesthetic practice of patching as a possibility of reparative contingency (Köppert 2021). By patching, which is applying the black-and-white photographs like patches, like plasters to the surface of the image, an intimacy and relationality is created between the images and the times and spaces they convey, but without these amalgamating or merging in a manner similar to an alloy. The aesthetic process of patching indicates that there is no seamless transition between images, structures, and surfaces. Dissonances remain between the things that connect, or rifts. According to Yusoff (2018, 63) rifts are the condition of survival in racially dehumanized worlds. The unwelded in the touch of the images forms the resonant space for what seems unavailable as the possibility of Black life in ruined landscapes. The unavailable articulates itself as probability in the unwelded, which is, after all, a touch. This sensual moment of touch in the photographs conveys, in my view, what cultural theorist Lauren Berlant means when they write that it would take a form "that intensifies one's attachment to the world felt but yet unestablished" (2016, 399). The touch that exhibits the rift and the incompatible can be interpreted as a felt intensification of what might have been. Touch affectively intensifies unrealized futures of the past in the present.

With the arrangement of Black people as human chains, for example, we can see the brutalization of the colonial system. However, we might also be reminded of the 1907 cobalt miners' strikes that art historian Siobhan Angus addresses in her article *Mining the History of Photography* (2021). In it, she discusses the complex interplay between the silver that had to be extracted to create silver gelatin for a photograph showing workers in Canada striking against the undignified conditions of cobalt mining. In Baloji's montages a past that could have been is invoked in a similar way by cutting collections of enslaved people in front of a mine so that they look as if they are lining up to strike. Thus, it could be argued that alongside the history of enslavement, a past is inscribed in the present of cobalt mining that may not have been, but feels as if it would not have been improbable. I think that with the incongruity of foreground and background montage becomes recognizable and touch is staged so that it becomes possible to connect with a world that is not developed but that can be felt in its potentiality against all odds. Thinking with cinema and media scholar Kara Keeling here is worthwhile. Keeling suggests that it would take an aesthetic mode to feel into the present what has always been there as the future of Blackness (2019, ix; 80). One can also think of Berlant's position that it is a kind of affective attention (attentiveness) that stands in the context of the genre of the ordinary and the supposedly incidental of macropolitical contexts, intensifying one's attachment to what has always been there but was never anchored as a reality of life (Berlant and Edelman 2014, 19). I would like to continue with David Shongo whose work enables in a similar, though different way to think futures past as an aspect of affect cultivated towards a change in recent climate politics.

Reparative Reading II: Touching the Future of Colonial Past
In *Bugs*, a photograph from the 2019 series *Blackout Poetry, Idea's Genealogy*, that I encountered in the realm of the exhibition *FIKTION KONGO. Kunstwelten zwischen Geschichte und Gegenwart* at Museum Rietberg: Kunst der Welt in Zurich (Switzerland), David Shongo mounts the body of a Congolese woman on the pattern of an electronic circuit board. It has been cut out of a historical portrait that the ethnologist and art dealer Hans Himmelheber had depicted in 1939 on his "research trip" to a village in the Cuba region of Congo (Guyer 2021). The original shows a square of a village that, like many others, had been built by the colonial occupiers from Belgium along specific hygiene guidelines to be able to increase the miners' output. At that time, they mined mainly copper in Congo, one of the most common materials used in the circuit board insinuated in the collage. In it, the conductors are silver,

again referencing the intertwining of photography and material extraction. At the same time, the presence of the extraction of raw materials for electronic production such as e-cars, as well as smartphones and computers, is shown to be a gendered history. The raw materialization of the female body since the beginning of colonization is crossed with the gendering of raw materials that supposedly offer themselves passively for penetration equaling extraction. The barcode mounted over the breast emphasizes the commodified nature of women's bodies as well as raw materials.

What interests me regarding this assemblage, which is produced in a way similar to Baloji's procedure as patching, is the relationship of the conflictual, which is produced by the touching of the layers as the potential of an alternative past to which it is necessary to relate affectively. The title of the collage is emblematic in this regard: bugs stand for program errors in programming and generate conflict within software technology insofar as they cause unexpected results and outputs. Embedded in the historical background of the collage, we are referred to the more cosmic than exact dimension of algorithms, and thus to the memory tablets Lukasa, which are important in the Katanga region.

As artifacts of communication that resemble computer mainboards, and thus the background of Shongo's collage, they can serve to decode Congolese history. What is crucial, however, is touching the mathematical map with one's fingertips. It takes touch to unlock knowledge. The features on the Lukasa, such as beads, shells, or pieces of metal, are not calculated purely cognitively, but interpreted affectively. From the western perspective of a still very cognitively derived understanding of algorithmization, such a mnemonic technique probably represents the bug. In the context of the collage, however, this bug seems to me to be the potential to affectively relate to the past in its potentiality. Invoking the pre-colonial history of the Luba via the patching-orchestrated means of touch as the future of colonial past is something I understand to be reparative, not because there could be healing here in the sense of going back to pre-colonial time, but because affective contingency emerges as a possibility for repair and care.

To briefly summarize what I have tried to tackle, let me go back to the beginning of my argument. With Brian Massumi we have learnt that an assumed future is felt into the present moment where politics are fostered based upon affective facts. In the realm of anthropogenic climate change we often/commonly experience the contrary: the reality of threat is not translated into

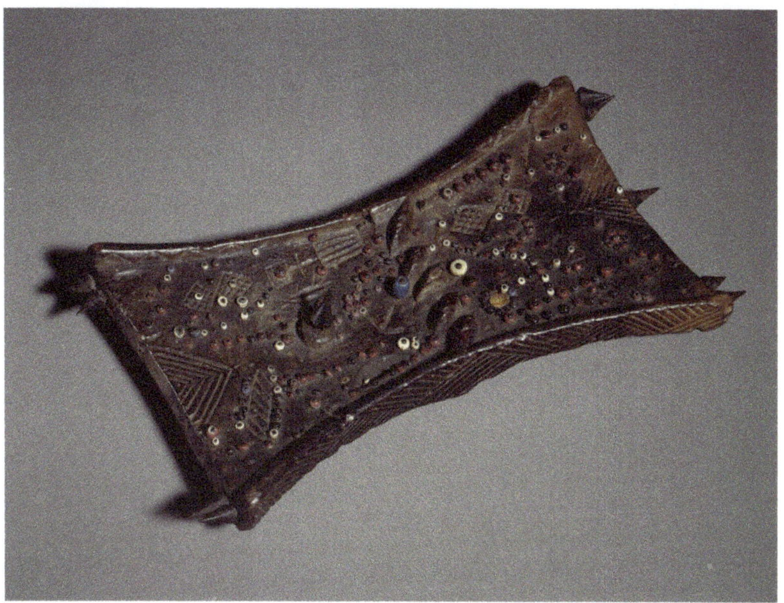

a felt one. Thus, politics are not under the pressure of a facticity that is being affective. Keeping this in mind, but also the
problem of the paranoia that had been developed due to the
affective fact of terrorist threat, I was wondering how affect
needs to be cultivated to finally interrogate the current climate
politics, but without the paranoia of imagining climate change
as disaster – since we know what the effects of paranoia are,
and that it is often the most marginalized that are hit.

Based on the photographs of Sammy Baloji and David Shongo,
I have therefore tried to show that, on the one hand, it should
be about counteracting anaesthetization by making aesthetics in the form of collage physical and material, and by using
such an understanding to explore the material dimension of
those that are most likely to be affected by unresponsiveness. In this way, the real conditions of colonial continuities
can also become clear where ecological values are supposed
to be sold with a smile on the face. But another argument is
important to me: instead of an affect oriented towards what
might be terrible in the future, we need a sense of affectively
connecting to the futures in the past of colonial extraction to
shape our present. What could have been must be felt in the
present. Because what could have been often starts where
most of the affective knowledge lies that we all need for the
immediate change of politics and habits. It is the affective
knowledge to perceive oneself within the web of systems that
animates worlds. The knowledge of those who were never

meant to survive, but nevertheless did due to the affective acknowledgment of this web describes the possibility in the impossibility (Keeling 2007). It is about protecting and supporting this knowledge and about forging complicity in difference, and utmost respect. With utmost respect because, of course, it should not be about exploiting "Africa as an imaginary reservoir of alternative and authentic realities" (McHardy et al. 2021, 15). Nothing about the colonial-historical and postcolonial conditions of climate change is to be romanticized, and yet we should be committed to the idea of acknowledging anti-hegemonic aesthetic methods – affectively, by which is meant not sentimentality but response-ability towards climate change.

Angus, Shioban. 2021. "Mining the History of Photography." In *Capitalism and the Camera: Essays on Photography and Extraction*, edited by Kevin Coleman and Daniel James, 55–73. London/New York, NY: Verso Books.

Berlant, Lauren. 2016. "The Commons: Infrastructures for Troubling Times." *Environment and Planning D: Society and Space*, 34 (3): 393–419.

Berlant, Lauren, and Lee Edelman. 2014. *Sex, or the Unbearable*. Durham, NC/London: Duke University Press.

Blickstein, Tamar. 2019. "Affects of Racialization." In *Affective Societies*, edited by Jan Slaby and Christian van Scheve, 152–65. London: Routledge.

Demos, T.J. 2017. *Against the Anthropocene: Visual Culture and Environment Today*. Berlin: Sternberg Press.

De Wet, Phillip. 2018. "Elon Musk's family once owned an emerald mine in Zambia – here's the fascinating story of how they came to own it." *Business Insider*. Accessed July 14, 2022. https://businessinsider.co.za/how-elon-musks-family-came-to-own-an-emerald-mine-2018-2.

Edwards, Elizabeth, 1992, *Anthropology and Photography, 1860-1920*. New Haven: Yale University Press

Edwards, Elizabeth and Christopher Morton (ed.), 2017, *Photography, Anthropology and History*. London: Routledge.

Fay, Jennifer. 2022. "Do I Know the Anthropocene When I See It?" *Representations* 157 (1): 41–67.

Guyer, Nanina. 2021. "Vorwärts in die Vergangenheit. Künstlerische Forschung und Mitautorenschaft in Hans Himmelhebers Fotografien aus dem Kongo 1938/39." *Fotogeschichte: Beiträge zur Geschichte und Ästhetik der Fotografie* 41 (162): 13–21.

McHardy, Julien et al. 2021. "Digital Imaginaries. Beyond Binaries." In *Digital Imaginaries. African Positions Beyond Binaries*, edited by Richard Rottenburg et al., 12–32. Bielefeld: Kerber.

Hartman, Saidiya V. 1997. *Scenes of Subjection: Terror, Self-Making, and Slavery in Nineteenth Century America*. Oxford: Oxford University Press.

Keeling, Kara. 2007. *The Witch's Flight. The Cinematic, the Black Femme, and the Image of Common Sense*. Durham, NC/London: Duke University Press.

Keeling, Kara. 2019. *Queer Times, Black Futures*. New York, NY: New York University Press.

Köppert, Katrin. 2021. "Rifted Algorithms. Digitale Medienkunst postafrikanischer Zukünfte." *Navigationen* 21 (2): 145–58.

Massumi, Brian. 2010. "The Future Birth of the Affective Fact." In *Affect Theory Reader*, edited by Melissa Gregg and Gregory J. Seigworth, 52–70. Durham, NC/London: Duke University Press.

Mirzoeff, Nicholas. 2014. "Visualizing the Anthropocene." *Public Culture* 26 (2): 213–32.

Morris, Rosalind C. and Daniel Eschkötter. 2019. "Versuchszonen des Spätindustrialismus. Goldabbau in Südafrika." *Zeitschrift für Medienwissenschaft* 11 (20): 78–95.

Quijano, Aníbal. 2016. *Kolonialität der Macht, Eurozentrismus und Lateinamerika*. Wien/Berlin: Turia+Kant.

Palmer, Tyrone S. 2017. "'What Feels More Than Feeling?' Theorizing the Unthinkability of Black Affect." *Critical Ethnic Studies* 3 (2): 31–56.

rnd. 2021. "Möglicher Wassermangel: Laschets und Musks Lachen entsetzt Bürgerinitiative." Accessed July 17, 2022. https://rnd.de/wirtschaft/armin-laschet-und-elon-musk-lachen-nach-wassermangel-frage-buergerinitiative-ist-entsetzt-CFKI3I7HKTAMIPRHE-JCN33B2GU.html.

Rodríguez Aguilera, Meztli Yoalli. 2021. "Everyday Resistances to Environmental Racism. Mestizo Geographies, and Toxicity in Oaxaca." *The Funambulist* 35: 48–53.

Sedgwick, Eve Kosofsky. 2003. "Paranoid Reading and Reparative Reading, or, You Are so Paranoid, You Probably Think This Essay is About You." In *Touching Feeling: Affect, Pedagogy, Performativity*, edited by Eve Kosofsky Sedgwick et al., 123–51. Durham, NC/London: Duke University Press.

Shotwell, Alexis. 2022. "Ethical Orientations Toward Repair in Climate Change." Accessed July 14, 2022. https://alexisshotwell.com/2022/04/.

Yao, Xine. 2021. *Disaffection. The Cultural Politics of Unfeeling in Nineteenth-Century America*. Durham, NC/London: Duke University Press.

Yusoff, Kathryn. 2018. *A Billion Black Anthropocenes or None*. Minneapolis, MN: University of Minnesota Press.

Operating Disaster:

Closing Discussion

Moderated by Marie Sophie Beckmann

The final agenda item of the "Records of Disaster" workshop provided for a roundtable. Organizers, presenters, and participating students gathered in a circle to draw together the thematic threads that ran through the contributions heard, seen, and discussed. Among them was the pressing question of what potential mass media and artistic images, records and documents hold for creating a critical, affective proximity to human-induced climate change that in turn results in real actions. For a "disaster," as one conclusion of the conversation might be formulated, is to be understood above all in terms of its operationality: It calls for immediate action.

Keywords: Mass Media, Climate Change, Artistic Research, Affect

151

Marie Sophie Beckmann: Welcome to our closing discussion. When the idea for this workshop came about, we started to think about disaster as an operative term in the sense that it allowed us to bring together different, often conflicting and disparate perspectives on environmental catastrophes, climate change, and the relationships between different materials and the social and political registers at work in these catastrophic events. I want to take this idea of disaster as a mode of operation in and of itself, as something that is transformative, by asking where exactly the operational potential of disaster lies? What does it do, but also what do we do with it? Or what does it allow us to do?

Jakob Claus: What was interesting for me yesterday and today is that disasters on the one hand can be grasped via a technical definition, as Gabriele Schabacher suggested; there can be a quantitative measurement of what counts as an accident. On the other hand, there is what Susan Schuppli refers to as climate change nostalgia, the feeling of loss when one sees the ice melting for example. It is a beautiful image, a powerful image, and as such it evokes a feeling of nostalgia, the imagination that there was once a time when the ice was pristine and perfect. In this respect I found Katrin Köppert's thoughts on paranoia especially inspiring as contrast and I'm wondering how the concept of paranoia might relate to nostalgia as a feeling or emotional map that is associated with experiencing and mediating disaster.

Katrin Köppert: Joseph Masco says that we are currently talking about the crisis in a way that immobilizes us.[1] I was thinking about the extent to which that applies to disaster: when our thinking is paranoid, it makes us feel like we are in a crisis. That would be Eve Kosofsky Sedgwick's idea, right?[2] That paranoia triggers the idea of always being driven by the catastrophic moment, as if it were an addiction. And within that dependency, it paralyzes rather than initiates change. And this is actually where nostalgia comes in. Sedgwick also refers to Wendy Brown,[3] who wrote an article about the left being nostalgic about its own past, in the sense that we need to go back to a time when politics was allegedly more effective. And it's that nostalgia that prevents us from reinventing what a left politics could mean. So, if we apply that to the issue of climate change or disaster, it would mean that when we think of disaster paranoia, in some ways it's about nostalgia, about always holding on to past policies that have led to us doing nothing. Nonetheless, I think it is important to have the term "disaster" in the room and in this workshop. Climate change has often been discussed in terms of slow violence and slow death. In

1   See Joseph Masco 2017.

2   See Eve Kosofsky Sedgwick 2003.

3   See Wendy Brown 2002.

this sense, it is important to use disaster as an operative term to make us feel that something really serious is happening and we need to affectively relate to it, but not in a paranoid way. That would block us again.

Petra Löffler: The term "disaster," as it appears in the title of the workshop, is of course a bit provocative, but the provocation is deliberate. I like the idea that an event that is called a disaster is seen as a call to action. And that ties into what you were saying, Katrin. When you are stuck in a situation, you have to act. "Disaster" is an ambivalent term that evokes some negative associations. But in a technical sense – and this is perhaps the operational aspect of the term – it calls for immediate action.

Charlotte Bolwin: I would fully agree that disaster is an operational and a strategic term, as Petra just explained. When you, Marie, asked us to think about what such an operational term can do, it struck me that it gives a political dimension to something that otherwise could only be described in very functional or radically objective terms, with words such as interrupting a process or causing a sudden change. Calling something a disaster, in turn, means calling up all the affective, cultural sociological, and of course very human and political dimensions that these events have.

Solveig Suess: I want to go back to a quote by Donna Haraway that is often mentioned, which is that not everything is connected to everything, but there are lines of connection that are important to untangle, especially when we articulate the urgency of the policies that we are talking about. It is not just a general change. It is a particular crisis, and also a really strange balancing act between over-spectacularization and over-dramatization; between having a great sense of urgency and at the same time finding the capacity and means to act. Rob Nixon has talked very clearly about slow violence and about temporal disjunction:[4] all the different mechanisms that occur in politics that create temporal disjunction and make it impossible to see or feel or understand anything beyond a certain scale. So how do you then create these alignments or certain lines to feel some kind of agency in this situation?

Xiamao Wang: I find it interesting because I think we take two positions. We are both responsible for the destruction of nature and the victims of that destruction.

Maia Giebeler: In my opinion, there are not two but three perspectives to see our role in this disaster. We are not only the

4   See Rob Nixon 2011.

victims and perpetrators, but also the ones who might be able to change the action. In a way, we are the helping hand.

Kristina Genrich: If I remember correctly, Petra and Jakob gave a definition in their introduction of disaster that says a disaster is an event where outside help is needed. Referring to climate change as a disaster is a pretty dystopian way of looking at it then, because in the end we are left with the reality that we cannot deal with the situation on our own. In that sense, I found that formulation very provocative.

Petra: That is the question: is there anyone who can help us from the outside? Is it a matter of leaving Earth behind and looking for another planet where we will make the same mistakes again? There is a kind of excess in thinking about this question of who can save us. If we are not able to save ourselves, who is?

Katrin: In terms of who the "otherworldly help" might be, Maia said that we are the victims, the perpetrators, and also the ones who could help, but I think there is another dimension to that. There are all these critters that are already doing their work, while we are still stuck in our state of shock. You might have read Anna Lowenhaupt Tsing's book *The Mushroom at the End of the World*, where she talks about the ways in which fungi are doing healing and repair work. So, in that way, we are already being helped.

Vanessa Barbagiovanni Bugiacca: Maybe we shouldn't think of outside help as "otherworldly," but rather as "out of the system"? Because it is a certain perspective and a certain way of life that creates all these problems.

Kristina: I really like that thought. To go back to what was said earlier, that we are aware of the problems and see the changes, but we still don't do anything, or at least not enough. At the end of the day, isn't that the question we are talking about? How to call humanity to action without triggering paranoia on the one hand, but on the other hand making it clear what kind of crisis we are in?

Charlotte: I think it is crucial to consider not just the disaster itself, but also the way in which it is documented and recorded. This is also what we have done in this workshop. Looking at artistic and media practices and understanding them as being situated in an environment that is a crisis on many levels: aesthetic, political, and epistemological. I also wanted to come back to a point that Katrin made in her talk, that the reason we are not affected by climate change is that we are affectively tied to the system that we are living in right now. We shouldn't forget that not changing something is also a choice. There is always a choice to do and want something different. So when we talk about why we don't act, we seem to forget that by staying tied to a capitalist, neoliberal lifestyle, we are, in fact, acting and making decisions every day.

Maia: I would like to focus on the other word of the title: records. I think it is somewhat a privilege for us to talk about disasters, since many other people don't have the time or the energy to deal with these issues.

Petra: So would you recommend more regulations of lifestyle, for instance paying for plastic bags in the supermarket, or more education in the broadest sense? I mean, that is one of the reasons why we wanted to work on these issues in the framework of a workshop with students, because we wanted to raise awareness about responsibilities.

Vico Rosenberg: I don't think it is about education, which of course is important. But the bigger issue is not to put all the responsibility on the individual. It is a structural problem, a problem caused by a capitalist system. For instance, I was in Ghana last year for two and a half months, and what you can see there is the other end of the infrastructure that we use here. The meat business in Ghana, for example, is completely dominated by the German meat market. So, we may be eating less meat, but we are still producing excess amounts that are being sent there. Conversely, the people in Ghana don't have the opportunity to do their own farming, and are deprived of the opportunity to earn their own money. So when we say that things are not changing here, we are only pretending that we as individuals can change things. There is a lot more happening at the top. But on the other hand, it is also wrong to leave everything to those "up there." It is difficult.

Fabian Becker: I have the impression that these crises seem to be too far away, which makes it hard for people to do or change something. It is only once it gets closer that more action is taken. We need to somehow bring it closer to people, maybe it should be 'promoted' more? That may be the wrong word for it, but hopefully you know what I mean. I really feel that this distance is often the big problem.

Katrin: But let's think about Fridays for Future and other similar initiatives. They were very present in the mainstream media, especially before the Ukraine war. Isn't it less about how they are portrayed in the mainstream and more about how we relate to that?

Fabian: It seems to me that there was still very little coverage. Of course, it was in the mainstream media. But I feel like when it comes to the scale of the crisis, climate change is not as present as some other issues. Also, Fridays for Future is aimed at the younger generation. But what about the older generations?

Kristina: I think that the media coverage of the climate crisis has been very good. When the COVID-19 pandemic broke out, there was less coverage, and a lot of the discussions died down. But what I think is important in this context is also the question of which issues were actually being discussed. I felt that the coverage of Greta Thurnberg or Fridays for Future was less about the crisis and more about things like: Oh, these kids aren't going to school. Shifting the focus like that is very problematic.

Jakob: Thinking about the difficulty of relating to disaster and climate change, personally for me it was very helpful to take on Susan Schuppli's notion of "critical proximity." One of my questions during the workshop was how this proximity can be perceived when the perspective changes. It is not about waiting for something to affect me, but about changing the way I might be affected. At least in the artistic contributions we have been discussing over the last two days, it became clear for me that this change in sensitivity or visibility can occur as soon as you conceive of material infrastructures as soft materials, as materials that are marked by catastrophe and are like a material proxy for the things we want to perceive and understand. To emphasize this connection between proximity on the one hand and material and witnessing on the other, which is always a form of softness, of change in dynamics that can be read but must first be trained – that's important.

Charlotte: In the conversation with Susan the proxy concept came up, I think, when talking about Timothy Morton and his notion of hyperobject.[5] He says that climate change is a hyperobject, that is, something that is beyond the immediate scope of human perception, or I think he would also say, reasonability or sensibility, because we cannot really grasp it as a whole if we apply our usual ways of thinking and perceiving. And yes, I like very much what you said that both the material witnesses like ice, sand, water, as well as the media documents could be something that we could discuss as a proxy that somehow bridges this gap between the abstract character of certain

5   See Timothy Morton 2013.

concepts such as climate change or Anthropocene and the sensual and perceptible registers that are called in it.

Kristina: I am not quite sure I understand the concept of critical proximity yet. Is it just a spatial proximity or could it also be something that is medially felt? And if so, could we also talk about material witnesses as a way to create that critical proximity, to connect people who are not in the vicinity of a disaster and make them feel closer, to realize the crisis mode?

Charlotte: I think the way you connected it is perfect. In the discussion we had with Susan she didn't directly connect the idea of critical proximity to the data proxy, but I would agree with you and follow your argument that mediating practices – whether it is directly, so to speak, when we are in the ice lab, but also when we are watching a film made in that lab – are very important. Susan was referring first to critical proximity when she was talking about nuclear waste placement, saying, "If you take it from Canada to Norway and dump it in the ocean there, it is far away only in terms of geological proximity."

Petra: I want to revisit the issue of mass media and its role in approaching climate change and the need to act against it. Perhaps mass media, and especially image-based mass media, play a delicate role in this. Katrin talked about aestheticization and anesthesia, and there has always been a debate in media theory about anesthesia through mass media, assuming if you consume too many images of information, you are no longer able to respond effectively to those images or information. Perhaps this is part of the problem: when you consume images, you can distance yourself from what you are seeing. Susan Sontag, for example, thought about this as well,[6] that we can consume images of extreme violence without being affected by the violence because we are safe as observers, as viewers. And we can also be kind of aroused or perversely enjoy these images of violence. Another part of the problem is that we have these very beautiful images of climate change. I am thinking, for example, of the photographs by Edward Burtynsky. He works with a very strong aerial view of the Earth, which looks very beautiful but also abstract, and places the viewer at an immense distance. So maybe images are indeed part of the problem. The worst part is probably that it is so common to consume images. Consequently, one solution could be images that are not so easy to consume, that even resist consumption – images that make you think and also make you act. And I understood your presentation, Katrin, to be going in that direction when you talked about the sense of touch and being touched.

6   See Susan Sontag 2003.

Katrin: Returning to the question of what critical proximity is, I wonder to what extent the first step could also be to understand materiality not as a passive witness of something, but also to understand materials as media in themselves and from there to come to the idea that these materials mediate the relationship between them and us. And whether that mediating moment, the proximity, can be a sought after one. Perhaps this could also be translated into the question of the extent to which records, like films and so on, can imitate the mediating processes of the material in a way that then works differently.

Charlotte: You asked if media imitate the material, and I find that very interesting. I would rather say it is an act of translation. Not in the sense of Latour, whose understanding of translation is very formal, but maybe in the sense of Walter Benjamin and situated within his aesthetic theory of language and translation, where there is a change of register in any translation process, but not an ontological one; rather a poetic opening, where some things don't correspond directly with each other, but somehow there still is a continuation.[7]

7   See Walter Benjamin's philosophy of language and translation, especially his essay *The Task of the Translator* (1996).

Jeike Zorn: I wanted to add something to the discussion about critical proximity: I have an impression that I find difficult to put into words, but after these two days I have had a shift in perspective of how I relate to climate change, in the sense that after seeing the ice in the film this morning, I also see myself more as material. It helped me to realize the ways in which I am a part of all of this.

Marie: That is a very nice thing to happen!

Vico: I wonder if we have reached a limit with mass media — and whether newer technologies like virtual reality have more potential to make one feel connected and to raise people's awareness. For example, when I put on VR goggles, I am in a different world, or at least I feel like I am. Maybe it is a chance to take some people to the South Pole and let them see what it looks like, what it sounds like, how endangered it is. I'm curious what your opinion is on this.

Solveig: At film festivals I often see these labs to support VR experiences, documentaries and things like that. But somehow I always feel like it falls short in some ways. Maybe it is also the experience of putting the headset on. It is heavy and clunky, or you feel dizzy if you sit in it too long. And there are pretty strict limitations on the format itself. All of that leads to a certain inadequacy or limitation of this medium. Also, I would not want to give up older forms of media so quickly, even the power of the collective experience of watching something together, or even the process of filmmaking itself, the collaboration, the very human context of it.

Marie: There are already efforts to somehow make tangible certain experiences that we find difficult to comprehend. For instance, there are interactive web-based games where players are invited to take on the role of a migrant, suggesting that this will create empathy.[8] I feel like these VR experiences you mentioned could go in a similar direction, but I don't think they create the kind of proximity that we are talking about. I also enjoyed what you said, Solveig, that we shouldn't forget how coming together in a space can also create something. Or what you just described, Jeike, this way of feeling differently about yourself and also thinking differently about how you relate to certain earthly materials.

Kristina: It seems as if we often look for technical means to create some kind of awareness or more proximity to all these problems and crises. I personally think that it is not always about the technology or the movies that we see, but a lot of times it is just that we humans are drowning in information and images. It is so difficult to find a way to show things that stick; people get so numb to these images that even if it hurts for a few days, it rarely gets to the point where it really sticks and leads to action. This is a problem that you cannot solve with new technologies.

Petra: The notion of experience seems to be in the room, especially in regard to an affective relation to climate change. Vico, you told us about your time in Ghana and how you experienced how the local meat market was affected by the globalized meat market. You saw a very concrete connection. And as you know, Susan Schuppli is not here because she is doing research in the Arctic. She is an artist and a researcher who, we could say, decided to go where the trouble is.[9] And staying with the problems is something that we can do even in smaller situations, in situations that are here. But I assume that it is important to think about experience as a way of being in the world, and also as a way of thinking critically.

Richard Kachel: We have discussed so many different places and channels, like VR, but we haven't discussed the aspect of time yet. If we take the case of climate change, we all know that most of the information has been there since the first paper by the Club of Rome in the early 1970s,[10] and it has also been in the media since then. So isn't it also important for how long information is around? We take in information until we are

8   See Nicole Braida 2022.

9   See Donna J. Haraway 2016.

10   See Donella H. Meadows et al. 1972.

overflowing with it. I wonder if it is easier to react to something short term like the war in Ukraine or the explosion in Beirut last year because it is, or seems, less abstract?

Solveig: The question then would also be how to connect events like the war in Ukraine or the explosion in Beirut with climate change – because they are indeed intertwined. Toxic capitalism, the various legacies of colonialism, all these forces come into play in this context. It is unfortunate that these events seem so isolated and easy to digest because in reality they are so far-reaching.

Charlotte: This makes me think of Jean-Luc Nancy's essay *After Fukushima: The Equivalence of Catastrophes*, in which Nancy says that disasters are not necessarily equal, but they are made equal because they are consumed in the same system of capitalist information, media, and consumerism. Jakob and I were talking this morning about common broadcast news and how they always play entertaining jingles after they, for instance, report from Sri Lanka where it is 50 degrees now, which is a disaster. But the presentation is very standardized. That also ties in with what Petra was saying about mass media, that it is an infrastructure that we know very well, something so commonplace that the question might be whether there is still a reflexive moment in there, or potential for connectivity.

Marie: Another topic that kept coming up is all these different techniques and ways of working with and on these documents and materials, how to make things visible and knowable. One of the guiding questions that was important in putting this program together was the question of analysis, and we learned about many different approaches today. There was the idea of reparative reading, of sensory ethnography, and in the conversation with Armin Linke the question came up of how to make certain phenomena, which are often acts of violence, visible and knowable without manifesting that violence. So I would like to come back to the possibilities and perhaps also the limits of these different concepts and tools that we have discussed today. How do we manage to negotiate different perspectives, and engage in critical debate?

Katrin: So far, we have talked about ourselves as the ones who look at images, who experience and consume images. But we are also the ones who do something, right? We write, we analyze, we produce. So yes, it is interesting and important to talk about methods. Reflecting on this would also avoid possibly creating a distance by saying that we are just consuming, whereas as scholars and students we indeed play a more active role.

Richard: I would say that in times of mass media, we have become so accustomed to passive consumption that even talking directly to someone becomes rare, something perhaps even difficult but also effective. You cannot just back out of a conversation. So I think conversation is the best way to make people aware.

Benjamin, Walter. 1996. "The Task of the Translator." In *Selected Writings Vol 1. 1913-1926*, edited by Marcus Bullock and Michael W. Jennings, 253–65. Cambridge, MA/London: Harvard University Press.

Braida, Nicole. 2022. *Migrating Through the Web: Interactive Practices About Migration, Flight and Exile*. Bielefeld: transcript.

Brown, Wendy. 2002. "Resisting Left Melancholia." In *Loss. The Politics of Mourning*, edited by Davin Eng and David Kazanjian, 458–66. Berkeley, CA: University of California Press.

Haraway, Donna J. 2016. *Staying with the Trouble: Making Kin in the Chthulucene*. Durham, NC/London: Duke University Press.

Masco, Joseph. 2017. "The Crisis in Crisis." *Current Anthropology* 48 (15): 65–76.

Meadows Donella H., Dennis L. Meadows, Jørgen Randers, and William W. Behrens III. 1972. *The Limits of Growth: A Report for The Club of Rome's Project on The Predicament of Mankind*. New York, NY: Universe Books.

Morton, Timothy. 2013. *Hyperobjects: Philosophy and Ecology after the End of the World*. Minneapolis, MN: University of Minnesota Press.

Nixon, Rob. 2011. *Slow Violence and the Environmentalism of the Poor*. Cambridge, MA: Harvard University Press.

Sedgwick, Eve Kosofsky. 2003. "Paranoid Reading and Reparative Reading, or, You're so Paranoid, You Probably Think This Essay is About You." In *Touching Feeling: Affect, Pedagogy, Performativity*, edited by Michèle Aina Barale, Jonathan Goldberg, Michael Moon, and Eve Kosofsky Sedgwick, 123–51. Durham, NC/London: Duke University Press.

Sontag, Susan. 2003. *Regarding the Pain of Others*. New York, NY: Picador.

Authors

Marie Sophie Beckmann is a postdoctoral research and teaching associate at the Institute for Art and Visual Culture at Carl von Ossietzky University of Oldenburg. She completed her doctorate in 2021 on the *Cinema of Transgression* as part of the DFG Research Training Program Configurations of Film at Goethe University Frankfurt.

Charlotte Bolwin is a research assistant and associate at the department of media at Bauhaus University Weimar, where she is working on a project on digital media art and aesthetics. Previously, she studied cultural studies (M.A.) and literary studies (B.A.) in Berlin and Paris.

Jakob Claus is a research associate at the Institute of Art and Visual Culture at Carl von Ossietzky University of Oldenburg where he is currently working on a PhD on the conditions of colonial and ecological knowledge production in early twentieth century ethnology. He studied cultural and media studies in Berlin, London and Lüneburg.

Katrin Köppert is Junior Professor of Art History/Popular Cultures at the Academy of Fine Arts in Leipzig, and was Substitute Professor for Transformations of Audiovisual Media at the Ruhr-Universität Bochum (2021–22). Her research interests include queer media theory, queer art and/of AI, gender, race and photography, and post-/decolonial (media) theories (of the Anthropocene in/and digital culture).

Armin Linke is a photographer and filmmaker whose work is dedicated to documenting human uses of technologies and knowledge. In a collective approach with other creatives, researchers and scientists, the narratives of his works expand on the level of multiple discourses. His research on the Anthropocene and the natural, technological and urban environment began with the *Anthropocene Observatory* project at Haus der Kulturen der Welt (HKW) in Berlin.

Petra Löffler is Professor of Theory and History of Contemporary Media at Carl von Ossietzky University of Oldenburg. Her particular research interests include postcolonial epistemologies and media ecologies in the Anthropocene with a special focus on coral reef histories, archival practices in the digital age, and material culture.

Gabriele Schabacher is Professor of Media and Culture Studies at the Johannes Gutenberg University Mainz. Her research interests include the media history of transport, mobility and infrastructure, cultural techniques of repair, regimes of urban surveillance, and seriality research.

Susan Schuppli is an artist-researcher based in the UK whose work examines material evidence from war and conflict to environmental disasters and climate change. Schuppli has published widely within the context of media and politics and is author of the book, *Material*

Witness: Media, Forensics, Evidence.
She is Director of the Centre for
Research Architecture, Goldsmiths
University of London and is an
affiliate artist-researcher and Board
Chair of Forensic Architecture.

Solveig Qu Suess works within the
fields of documentary film, art and
research. Her practice is dedicated
to addressing the challenges of
representation in an increasingly
calculated world, where capital,
information and environments are
enmeshed within regimes of power
and control. Her research sits on the
intersections of visual ethnography,
environmental humanities and feminist science and technology studies.
She is currently a junior researcher
at Critical Media Lab, FHNW Basel
and a PhD candidate in Urban Studies at the University of Basel.